Bill Severn's Magic
with Rope, Ribbon,
and String

BILL SEVERN'S MAGIC WITH ROPE, RIBBON, AND STRING

Bill Severn
Illustrations by John Garcia

STACKPOLE BOOKS

Published by
STACKPOLE BOOKS
5067 Ritter Road
Mechanicsburg, PA 17055

Printed in the United States of America

10 9 8 7 6 5 4 3 2 1

First paperback edition, 1994.

Originally published in hardcover by David McKay Company, Inc.,
in 1982.

Cover design by Christine Mercer

Library of Congress Cataloging-in-Publication Data

Severn, Bill.
    [Magic with rope, ribbon, and string]
    Bill Severn's magic with rope, ribbon, and string / Bill Severn. –
1st paperback ed.
        p.   cm.
    Previous ed. : Magic with rope, ribbon, and string. © 1982.
    Includes index.
    ISBN 0-8117-2533-2
    1. Tricks–Juvenile literature. 2. Rope–Juvenile literature.
3. Knots and splices–Juvenile literature. I. Severn, Bill. Magic
with rope, ribbon, and string. II. Title. III. Title: Magic with
rope, ribbon, and string.
GV1559.S47   1994
793.8–dc20   93-17893
                                                                  CIP
                                                                  AC

CONTENTS

INTRODUCTION

You show both hands empty, clap them together, and suddenly produce a rope, or you start to cut a rope and it mysteriously vanishes and then reappears. Instead of a rope, you magically produce a streamer of bright red ribbon from an empty hand held high above your head, or you conjure up a ribbon out of a little circle of black paper that looks far too small to have hidden it.

Those are just some of the surprises in a whole chapter of quick and unusual opening tricks this book will teach you how to do. After you have caught the attention of your audience, you may want to show some of the tricky-knot routines, such as the one in which you instantly tie a knot with one hand, make it look like a pair of old-fashioned "spectacles," then change that knot into two others.

There are penetration tricks with fresh magical plots, disco records, or a bar of soap; with a coffee cup that instantly links itself to a rope, or where a whole batch of rings falls from a ribbon at a spectator's command. You will find a variety of the ever-popular cut and restored effects to choose from, other tricks in which ropes and ribbons stretch, grow long or short, or join together, or in which they seem to defy gravity or suddenly become acrobatically alive.

Most of the tricks are do-anywhere magic. Those with rope or ribbon are visible enough to be shown to almost any group, large or small, and there are other tricks and routines with string for close-up performances. The props are inexpensive, easy to assemble and to carry around, and ropes, ribbons, and strings are familiar to everyone as ordinary everyday objects. Sometimes, of course, they may not be as "ordinary" as the audience assumes, since they must be specially prepared in advance to accomplish the magic. But all the things required for the tricks in this book can be put together at home with commonly available materials.

What Rope to Use

The rope magicians use for most rope tricks is soft white clothesline. Dealers in magic equipment supply a kind specially designed for magical uses, since most clothesline, as it comes from the factory, is too hard and stiff to use. But there are types of ordinary clothesline and sash cord, generally available at hardware and variety stores, that will serve just as well if the inner core is removed to make them soft, pliable, and easy to cut through.

What is needed is one of the many brands manufactured with a "braided jacket," usually identified on the label as such. The best for magical purposes are those with what is called a "solid braided cotton jacket," but others with braided plastic jackets also can be used.

The braided jacket is an outer tube-like shell. Inside it, running through the whole length of the rope, is a core of several strands of string or twisted plastic fiber. Removing the core is simply a matter of pulling out the center strings, so that you are left with the braided outer jacket to use for rope tricks. The stripping process is not difficult.

How to Remove the Core

Cut a piece of braided-jacket clothesline to the desired length. Take one end of the line in your left hand, and use your right fingers to pull apart the braiding of the outer jacket at that end until about an inch of the inner core is exposed. Close your left hand around the jacket just beneath the same end and grip the core strings tightly with your right fingers. Now pull the strings up with your right hand as you slide the jacket down with your left hand.

After you have pulled out a few inches of the core, you will find that the jacket bunches so it is hard to pull out any more. When that happens, move your left hand to grip the jacket just below where it has bunched. Pull your left hand down along the whole length of the rope, to draw the bunched jacket down toward the bottom end so part of the jacket gradually becomes an empty tube at the bottom.

Continue in this manner, pulling out a few inches of the core, smoothing the jacket down toward the bottom, and then pulling out a few more inches of the core, until the entire outer jacket has been stripped free of the core. Trim off the two ends and your rope is ready to use.

Binding the Ends

If you plan to use the same length of rope repeatedly for a particular trick, you may want to bind the ends to keep them from fraying. The easiest way is simply to wrap a short strip of white cloth adhesive tape horizontally around each end. The ends also can be bound by coiling white cotton thread tightly around them and tying it off with small knots, or by stitching the ends with needle and thread.

Another way to bind the ends is to treat each of the ends with white craft glue, working it in well with your fingers, then rolling the ends to reshape them. Allow the white glue to dry and harden thoroughly before the rope is used.

Whether the ends are bound or not, there is a limit to how often the same piece of rope can be used before it becomes soiled and ragged-looking. Old rope should be kept for practice, but reasonably fresh and clean rope should be used for public performances.

Colored Ropes and Cords

For tricks requiring colored ropes, an easy and practical way to color short lengths of cotton-jacket clothesline is with felt-tip marking pens. Longer lengths can be colored with fabric paints, available at craft and hobby shops.

There are a variety of braided colored cords manufactured for upholstery and drapery uses that will serve many magical purposes. They can be bought in different thicknesses and textures, some hard-finished and others soft and loosely braided. Another substitute for colored rope is the thick rope-like yarn made in many colors for needlework projects and as ties for gift packages.

Ribbons

Silk ribbon, traditionally used by magicians for ribbon tricks, is no longer available in most shopping areas and, if it can be found, it is quite expensive. A serviceable substitute for use in "silk ribbon" tricks is polyester satin ribbon. While it lacks some of the springy compressibility of real silk, polyester satin ribbon is brightly colored, has a silky-smooth finish, and can be bought by the yard or in pre-packaged lengths and widths at almost any variety store.

If ribbon with a less slippery finish is needed, you may prefer to use grosgrain ribbon, which has a cross-ribbed surface, or sturdy cotton or rayon binding tape.

Magic Strings

Venetian blind cord makes an excellent "string" for most string tricks. The most common variety, which is best for magic, has an outer braided cotton jacket similar to cotton-jacketed clothesline. For most magic purposes this cord can be used as packaged, but if you wish an even softer and more pliable "string," the core can be removed in the same way as from rope. Venetian blind cord is white, provides good visibility, is strong, smooth to handle, and doesn't kink or ravel as many loose-stranded strings do.

There is also a variety of small-diameter upholstery cords available in many colors and finishes. As a general rule, it is probably better to use some form of braided cord for string tricks rather than strand-twisted string or twine, unless there is a specific reason for using the latter. If twine is to be used, jute may be best. Sisal twine should be avoided because of its splintery rough finish and entangling ragged strands.

MAGIC WITH ROPE, RIBBON, AND STRING

1

SUDDENLY A ROPE

The following tricks are for "openers." They are surprising or amusing ways to introduce a routine of rope or ribbon magic. Most of them are over in a minute, but in that minute they should help you to catch the attention of your audience and to make them want to see more.

CLAP HANDS!

How it looks

You hold both hands out at your sides to show

CLAP HANDS!

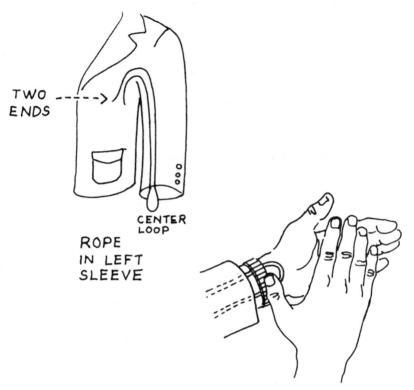

TWO ENDS

CENTER LOOP

ROPE IN LEFT SLEEVE

AS HANDS CLAP TOGETHER THUMB HOOKS LOOP

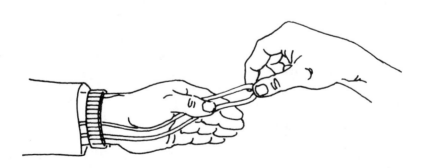

RIGHT HAND DRAWS ROPE UP THROUGH LEFT

that they're empty, clap them together in front of you, then draw them apart to produce a rope between them.

What you need

A 3½-foot length of soft rope.

You will also need to wear a wristwatch on your left wrist.

The secret

The rope is hidden up your sleeve, fixed so you can catch a loop of it with your thumb to draw it out through your hand and bring it suddenly into view. As simple as the method is, the effect is quite surprising.

Double the rope to bring its two ends together, then take the *center loop* and feed it down the left sleeve of your jacket from the inside armhole. Reach up into your sleeve and draw the center loop down until you can slide it beneath the band of your wristwatch, so the loop lies against the inside of your left wrist and extends about an inch beyond the watchband.

Hold the loop in place against your left wrist with your right thumb and stretch your left arm out full-length in front of you. Remove your right thumb from the loop and let your left arm drop to your side.

Inside, under your jacket, the two ends of rope should now hang a few inches over the armhole and down your left side. With the rope fixed that way, you can wear it safely until you are ready to do the trick, with no fear that it will fall down out of your sleeve.

What you do

Stand facing the audience with both hands naturally at your sides. Lift both hands *slightly* to show them empty by turning the palms outward. Turn your body a little to the right as you continue to raise your hands to waist level, so the back of your left hand is toward the audience.

Clapping your hands together is what puts them in position for secretly catching hold of the rope. The tip of your left thumb should point up toward the ceiling, the tips of the fingers toward the right. Bring your right palm against the left so the right fingers are vertical and the tip of the right thumb extends to the inside of your left wrist.

Clap your hands together twice, loudly, as if applauding. As you clap them the second time, catch the tip of your right thumb in the loop and draw the rope up through your left hand and out to the right, to bring it suddenly into view.

All the movements should blend together without any pause. There is nothing difficult about it, but it takes a little practice to do smoothly.

OVERHEAD RIBBON PRODUCTION

How it looks

Hold your left hand high above your head, palm toward the audience, fingers straight up and opened wide. Bringing your right hand up to it, tap a pointing finger against your left palm, quickly close your left hand, and instantly produce a long red ribbon.

What you need

A 3½-foot length of red satin ribbon, ½ inch wide.

A piece of thin cardboard cut from an index card to a size of 2½ by 3½ inches.

Transparent tape.

The secret

The cardboard is made into a small tube, shut at one end, which fits tightly on the tip of the second finger of your right hand. The ribbon is hidden in the tube, and your finger secretly snaps the tube into the left palm in the instant you bring your hands together above your head to produce the ribbon. The magical surprise of this quick opening trick depends on the unusual overhead position of your hands and the speed with which it is performed.

To make the tube, turn your right palm toward you and place one of the narrow ends of the cardboard against the inside of your second finger, with the left edge of the cardboard at the finger's middle joint. Wrap the cardboard into a tube around the finger as *tightly* as you can. Fasten it with a strip of tape and remove the tube from your finger. Pinch the left end of the tube flat and tape that end shut. Fasten another strip of tape horizontally along the seam of the tube.

Start with one end of the ribbon and pack it into the tube in little accordion folds, pushing them well down into the bottom with the tip of the little finger. When you come to the other end of the ribbon, leave an inch of that sticking up out of the tube.

OVERHEAD RIBBON PRODUCTION

CARDBOARD

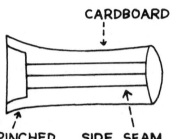

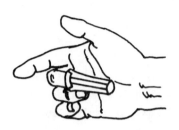

END PINCHED
FLAT_TAPED
SHUT

SIDE SEAM
TAPED

FITS TIGHTLY ON TIP
OF RIGHT SECOND FINGER

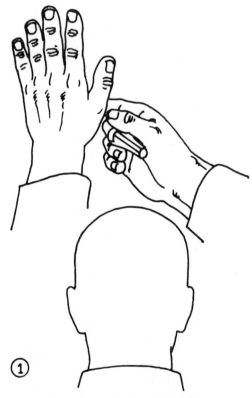

① POINTING RIGHT FINGER
TAPS RAISED LEFT PALM

LEFT HAND
TILTS
FORWARD
AND DOWN

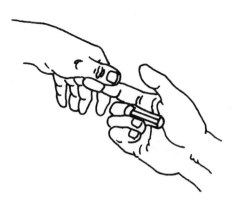

②

SECOND
FINGER
PUTS TUBE
INTO LEFT
PALM

③

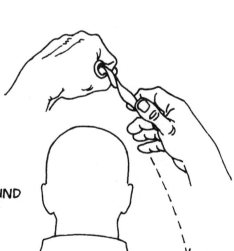

LEFT HAND
CLOSES AROUND
TUBE _ RIGHT
PULLS OUT
RIBBON

④

Now, if you jam the second finger of your right hand down into the tube as far as it will go, the tube should fit on that fingertip like a big tight thimble. The top end of the ribbon is between the finger and the inside of the tube, so that when you pull out your finger, the end of the ribbon is drawn out with it.

You can carry the ribbon-loaded tube in the right-hand pocket of your jacket or slacks, or you can have the tube on your table hidden behind some other prop. Just before you are ready to perform the trick, secretly fix the tube in position on the tip of your right hand's second finger. Stand with your right hand naturally at your side, with the back of that hand toward the audience and the fingers closed against the palm to conceal the tube from front view.

What you do

Raise your left hand straight up above your head, palm to the audience, thumb to the right, fingers toward the ceiling and spread open wide. Bring your right hand, with its back to the audience, up from your right side, up in front of your body, and up to the left hand raised above your head. Point with your right hand's first finger, keeping the other fingers closed back against the palm to conceal the tube. Tap your pointing first finger against your left palm just below the crotch of the left thumb.

The following moves should all blend together, quickly and smoothly, without any pause. Keep the tip of your right first finger touching your left palm near the crotch of the left thumb and tilt your left hand forward and down until its fingertips point to the floor. Straighten out your right second finger to bring the hidden tube up against the left palm. Close the left fingers into a fist around the tube and pull your right second finger from the tube, drawing out the end of the ribbon to grip it between that finger and the right thumb.

With your right hand, continue to pull the ribbon straight down from your raised and fisted left hand, until the full length of it is stretched downward between both hands. Hold it that way a moment, then drop the end of it from your left hand and let that hand fall to your side as your right hand holds up the suddenly produced ribbon.

You can get rid of the little tube that is hidden in your left hand by reaching into the left pocket of your jacket to bring out a ring, a pair of scissors, or whatever small prop you may be about to use in your ribbon routine, leaving the tube behind in the pocket. If you are not planning to use the produced ribbon in another trick, simply gather it up into your left hand, put it away in your left pocket, and leave the tube there with it.

SIGNS OF MAGIC

How it looks

You open out a small folded cardboard sign and hold it up with both hands so the audience can read it, and also so they can see there is nothing else in the folded sign as you show first the front and then the back. On the front, the sign reads: IT HAPPENS, and on the back: LIKE MAGIC! You close the folder, reach into it, and magically produce a rope.

What you need

An 8- by 14-inch piece of white poster board or other white cardboard.

A second piece of cardboard, 2½ by 5 inches.

A 3½-foot length of soft braided clothesline with its core removed.

Scissors or a sharp-pointed knife.

A paper stapler.

A pencil, ruler, black crayon or marking pen, and dull-finish transparent tape.

The secret

The folded rope is held in a small tube-like container which is stapled to the bottom front of the sign where your covering fingers hide it as they hold up the sign.

Place the cardboard on a table with its long edges top and bottom. Measure 7 inches in from the left side and draw a faint vertical pencil line down that center. Run the point of the scissors or knife down that line from top to bottom to score it. Fold the cardboard in half from left to right, press the fold flat, and open it out again. Reinforce the center fold, front and back, with vertical hinge-like strips of tape.

Turn the cardboard to its original position on the table. On the left half, measure 4 inches down from the top edge and draw a faint horizontal pencil line across. The base of the printed letters should be at that line. Because of the length of some of the

SIGNS OF MAGIC

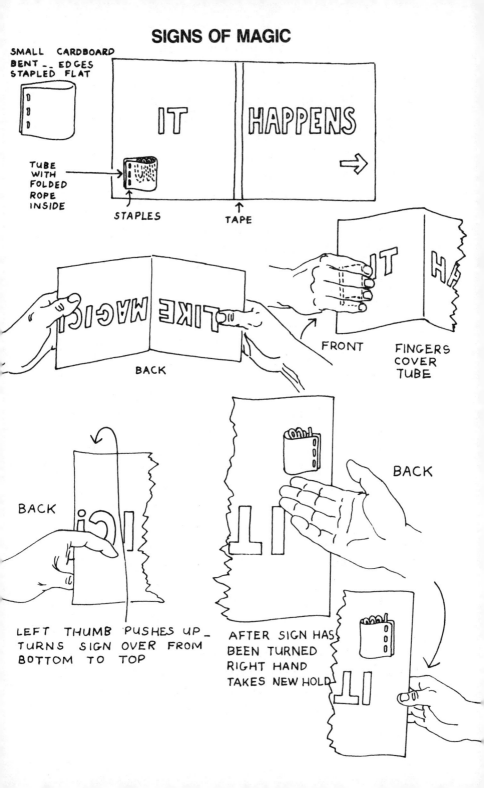

SMALL CARDBOARD
BENT -- EDGES
STAPLED FLAT

IT HAPPENS →

TUBE
WITH
FOLDED
ROPE
INSIDE

STAPLES

TAPE

LIKE MAGIC

BACK

FRONT

FINGERS
COVER
TUBE

BACK

BACK

LEFT THUMB PUSHES UP -
TURNS SIGN OVER FROM
BOTTOM TO TOP

AFTER SIGN HAS
BEEN TURNED
RIGHT HAND
TAKES NEW HOLD

words, the lettering should be kept tall and thin, but large enough for the audience to read it at a glance. Block out the letters with pencil and fill them in with black crayon or marking pen.

On the left side, print: IT. On the right side print: HAPPENS. Beneath the word HAPPENS, draw an arrow pointing to the right. Turn the cardboard over from *top to bottom*. (This is so the printing on the back will be right side up when you later turn the card while performing.) On the left half of the back, print: LIKE. On the right half, print: MAGIC!

Put the big piece of cardboard aside for a moment and turn the smaller piece so its long edges are at top and bottom. *Bend* the cardboard in half from right to left, to bring the two side edges together at the left, but *do not fold it flat*. Fasten those two edges flatly together with three vertically spaced staples. Press the center bend with your thumb to spread the sides and round it slightly.

Place the large cardboard with the word IT now facing you upright at the left. At a point ½ inch in from the left edge and an inch up from the bottom, attach the flat part of the small tube vertically to the large cardboard with three staples. Turn the cardboard over and cover the parts of the staples that have come through it with a vertical strip of tape. (This is to avoid scratching your fingers with the ends of the staples when handling the sign.) Again turn the cardboard to the side with the attached tube.

Fold the coreless clothesline back and forth upon itself in tight 2-inch accordion folds and leave the end of rope sticking up about ¼ inch above the rest of the folds. Squeeze the folds together and push the

entire folded rope down inside the tube from the top.
Close the folding sign from left to right.

If you plan to use this as an opening trick, you
can have the folder in your hands as you enter. Otherwise, rest it on the table with the open part to the
rear.

What you do

Hold the closed folder upright with your left
hand around the spine, thumb at the back, fingers in
front, and with its open edges toward the right. Put
your right hand inside, around the right edge near
the bottom, thumb at the back, and cover the tube
with your slightly arched fingers. Move your left
hand across the front of the folder, put your left fingers inside at the bottom right, and open it out between your hands to show that side of it. Hold it long
enough for the audience to read the printed words.

You are now about to turn the opened-out sign
over *forward* to show the other side. Do this by
bringing your left first finger to the back, placing
the nail of the left thumb against the front, and
pushing up with the thumb to pivot the whole thing
over from *bottom to top*. As the quick turnover is
completed, simply open your right fingers and lift
that hand away for an instant, then grip the right
edge of the sign again. Hold it between your hands
for the audience to read the printing that now faces
them.

With your left hand, shut the folder toward you
from left to right. Slide your left hand to the top
right corner. Put your left first finger between the
two edges and, with the other left-hand fingers at
the front and thumb at the back, turn the folder to

the left until its spine is toward the floor and the open edges are at the top. Hold it that way with your left hand.

Snap your right-hand fingers, show that the hand is empty, and reach inside the folder. Grip the end of the rope, pull it *down* from the tube to the inside bottom of the folder, and then draw it *slowly* out of the folder to the right.

The same folder could be used to produce yards of ribbon instead of rope, since the tube will hold much more ribbon than rope, or you might want to use it to produce several silk handkerchiefs.

INSTANT ROPE

How it looks

You take out a pair of scissors, show both hands empty, tap the top of your left fist with the scissors, and instantly produce from that hand a 4-foot length of rope.

What you need

A 4-foot length of soft clothesline with its core removed.

Scissors that will fit into a jacket pocket. The blades of the scissors should be about 3 inches long, from their tips to the screw at the center.

The secret

This trick is based on a standard method magicians use for producing a silk handkerchief with the aid of a wand. In this case, the rope is wound into a small ball around the blades of the scissors and is hidden by the natural transfer of the scissors from hand to hand as each hand is shown empty. It is very simple to perform but provides a quick surprise and a magical way of introducing the rope for a cut-and-restored rope trick.

Turn the closed scissors with the points toward the bottom and lay one end of the rope vertically on top of the blades. Wind the rope around the scissors point in flat lateral turns, making about five turns and then winding the next five flatly upon the first ones, and so on, until all of the rope is wound. Tuck the last end of the rope in under one of the wound strands to hold the ball together. Put the scissors, handle end down, into the right-hand pocket of your jacket.

What you do

Reach into your pocket with your right hand. Close your fingers loosely around the little ball of rope, and bring out the scissors with the back of your hand toward the audience. The scissors handles are at the top as you hold the scissors by their blades, and the screw at the center lies against the inside of your first finger.

What you do now should look as though you are simply transferring the scissors from hand to hand, to show first one hand and then the other empty.

Show your left hand empty and then turn its palm toward you, with its back to the audience. Bring your right hand to the left hand, right fingers inside the left. Slide the center of the scissors under your left thumb, which grips them there. Take your

INSTANT ROPE

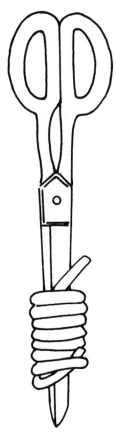

ROPE WOUND
AROUND SCISSORS

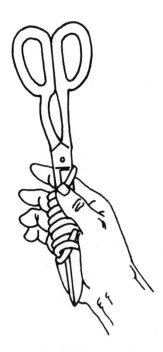

RIGHT HAND _ AFTER TAKING
SCISSORS FROM POCKET

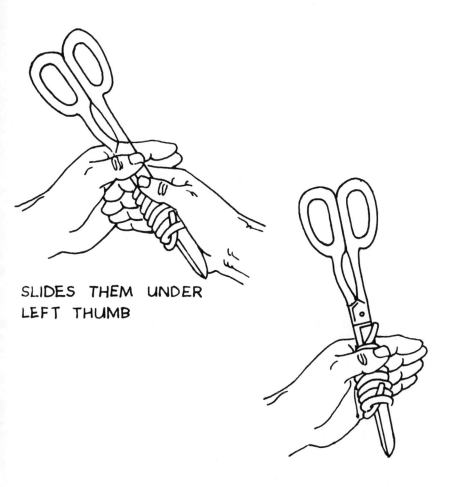

SLIDES THEM UNDER
LEFT THUMB

LEFT HAND HOLDS SCISSORS

SCISSORS REMOVED _
BALL OF ROPE REMAINS IN HAND

right hand away and close your left fingers around the scissors and ball of rope.

Show your right hand empty. Take the scissors handles with your right hand and draw the scissors up out of your left fist, leaving behind the hidden ball of rope. Hold the scissors high with your right hand, snip them in the air a couple of times, then tap them to the top of your left fist. Take the end of the rope between your right first finger and right thumb and draw it up out of your left hand, stretching the rope to full length between your hands as it magically comes into view.

CIRCLE AROUND A RIBBON

How it looks

You show both sides of a small circle of black paper and show both hands empty. Then you quickly fold the circle into a cone and magically produce a long bright-colored ribbon from it.

What you need

A circle 7 inches in diameter, cut from a sheet of black construction paper.

A 3½-foot length of bright-colored satin ribbon, ½ inch wide.

Transparent tape.

The secret

The ribbon is accordion-folded and banded around with a strip of transparent tape, sticky side out, which is fastened to part of the paper circle in a position where your fingers naturally cover it while showing that side of the circle.

Fold the ribbon back and forth upon itself in flat and even 2-inch accordion folds. Turn the folded ribbon to a horizontal position. Take a 3-inch strip of transparent tape and wrap it in a flat band vertically around the ribbon, with the tape's *sticky side out*.

Fold the paper circle in half from top to bottom, then in half from left to right. Crease the folds with your thumbnail, and open the paper again. Attach the folded ribbon by its band of tape to the lower right section of the circle, centered about ¾ inch in from the circle's outer rim. Now take another short piece of tape and fasten that, *sticky side down*, exactly over the tape that bands the ribbon. (This is done so the paper won't stick together when it is folded and carried among your other props.)

Have the circle on your table, folded from top to bottom so that the ribbon is hidden inside toward the rear at the right.

What you do

Slide your right hand in under the top fold of the circle so your fingers flatly cover the ribbon. With your right thumb outside at the back, pick up the circle between thumb and fingers, hold it upright, and shake it open to show the audience the front side of it. Show your left hand empty.

Turn your right hand over toward you, turning the circle over toward you from top to bottom, and immediately take what is now the top between your left thumb and first finger. Remove your right hand as your left hand holds up the circle to show that side to the audience.

CIRCLE AROUND A RIBBON

①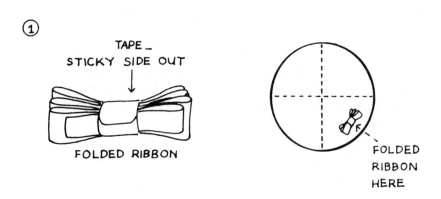

TAPE —
STICKY SIDE OUT

FOLDED RIBBON

FOLDED
RIBBON
HERE

②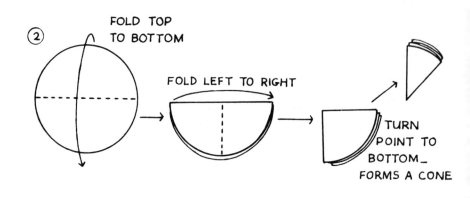

FOLD TOP
TO BOTTOM

FOLD LEFT TO RIGHT

TURN
POINT TO
BOTTOM —
FORMS A CONE

③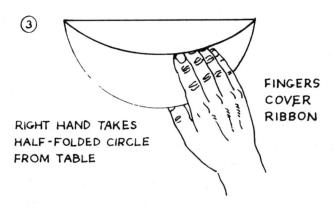

FINGERS
COVER
RIBBON

RIGHT HAND TAKES
HALF-FOLDED CIRCLE
FROM TABLE

BACK VIEWS

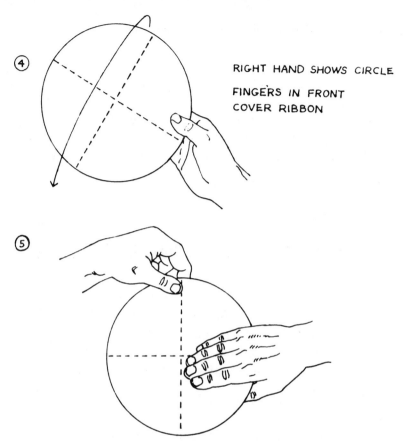

RIGHT HAND SHOWS CIRCLE

FINGERS IN FRONT
COVER RIBBON

RIGHT HAND TURNS IT OVER TOWARD
YOU FROM TOP TO BOTTOM _ THEN
LEFT HAND TAKES AT TOP

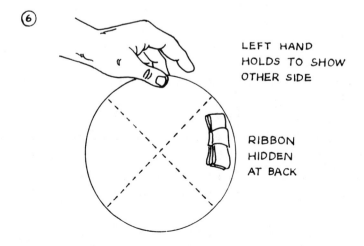

LEFT HAND
HOLDS TO SHOW
OTHER SIDE

RIBBON
HIDDEN
AT BACK

Bring your right hand to the outside center of the circle and quickly close it on its creases into the form of a cone. Hold the bottom point of the cone with your left hand, reach inside with your right hand, grasp the end of the ribbon, and pull it out to the side and then straight up to produce it from the cone.

THE ROPE THAT WASN'T THERE

This amusing opening effect starts as if you were about to perform a cut-and-restored-rope trick, but it turns to magical comedy as the rope suddenly vanishes and then, just as unexpectedly, reappears.

How it looks

"A little magic with a piece of rope," you say, as you show a rope in your left hand, "and a pair of scissors." You hold up the scissors with your right hand. "I shall now cut the rope." But as you speak, the rope instantly vanishes, leaving your left hand empty.

Pretending to be surprised, you stare at your empty hand, then look down at the floor, as though wondering where the rope went. "Well, if I *did* have a rope," you say, "I would take it by the center and cut it in half, so there would be two pieces."

You go through the motions without any rope, demonstrating in pantomime what you would do. "And then I would wrap it around my hand, say the magic words, and pull it out ... fully restored in one piece again." Suddenly, the vanished rope reappears, stretched between your hands. "Hey, there it is!" you say. "I knew I had a rope somewhere."

What you need

Two ropes with their cores removed, each 2½ feet long.

A 3½-foot length of strong white string or cord. (Any strong string will do, but the best to use is Venetian blind cord, size 4½.)

A pipe cleaner.

A small safety pin.

Scissors that will fit in your jacket pocket.

The secret

The first rope vanishes by means of what magicians call a "pull," that is, a string that pulls it up your sleeve. The duplicate rope, rolled into a ball, is hidden under the edge of your jacket where your fingers can secretly reach it when your hand is at your side.

Take one of the ropes, double it so the two ends touch together, and tie one end of the string *tightly* to the center loop. At the other end of the string, make a large slip-knot loop (see page 26). Slide your right hand through this loop and tighten the slip-knot to fasten that end of the string to your right forearm just above the top edge of your shirt cuff. Pass the string around your back, hold the ends of the rope in your left hand, and put on your jacket.

The string, tied to the center of the rope, now passes up the inside of your left sleeve, across your back, and down the inside of your right sleeve to where the other end is fastened to your right arm.

THE ROPE THAT WASN'T THERE

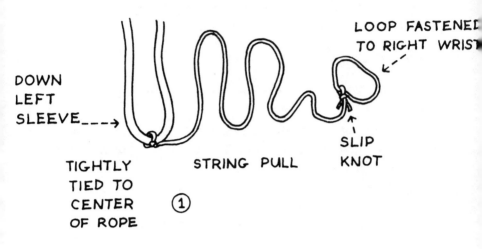

LOOP FASTENED TO RIGHT WRIST

DOWN LEFT SLEEVE────→

TIGHTLY TIED TO CENTER OF ROPE

STRING PULL

SLIP KNOT

①

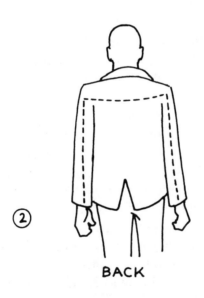

②

BACK

STRING UP LEFT SLEEVE, ACROSS BACK, DOWN RIGHT

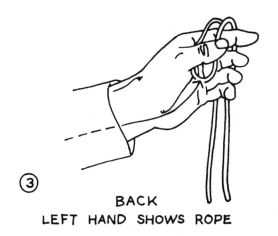

③ **BACK**
LEFT HAND SHOWS ROPE

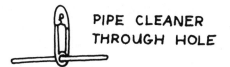

PIPE CLEANER
THROUGH HOLE

④ **ENDS BENT**
DOWN

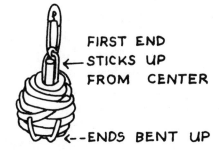

FIRST END
← **STICKS UP**
FROM CENTER

←-**ENDS BENT UP**

⑤

BALL OF ROPE ON
HOLDER UNDER
JACKET

To understand how the "pull" works, hold your left hand in front of your waist, with its palm toward you. Draw the rope and attached string through your left hand until you can grip the center of the rope between your thumb and first finger. Hold it there and suddenly swing your right hand up and out to the right. The doubled rope, pulled by the string, instantly shoots up your left sleeve out of sight. (You will have to experiment a little to decide how long the string should be, since that depends on the length of your arms. But once you have adjusted it correctly, you can use the same rope and string whenever you perform the trick.)

The duplicate rope is held under the bottom edge of your jacket by a holder made of a pipe cleaner and safety pin. Turn the safety pin so its clasp is at the top. Thread the pipe cleaner through the little hole at the bottom of the pin and bend the cleaner down until its two ends touch.

Place one end of the second rope vertically against the top of the pipe cleaner. Wind the rest of the rope into a small ball around its center, and tuck the last end of rope in under a wound strand to hold it tightly together. Bend up the two bottom ends of the pipe cleaner to keep the ball from sliding off.

Put on your jacket. Drop your two hands to your sides. Without moving your left arm, bend only your fingers up under the bottom edge of your jacket to the inside. Where your fingers touch the lining is the proper place to pin the holder with its ball of rope.

With the holder in place and the "pull" correctly adjusted, draw the rope down out of your left sleeve. Turn the palm of your left hand toward you and hold the center of the rope between your thumb and first finger, so the string runs through your partly closed hand. Since this is intended as an opening trick, you will have the rope set that way in your hand when you come out before your audience. The scissors should be in your right-hand jacket pocket.

What you do

While saying, "A little magic with a piece of rope," show the rope in your left hand and take the scissors from your pocket with your right hand. As you say, "And a pair of scissors," swing your right hand up high and out to the right to display the scissors. That pulls the string so the rope shoots up your left sleeve and vanishes. But pay no attention to your left hand. Hold it as it was and keep looking at the scissors. Snip them in the air and say, "I shall now cut the rope."

Then look at your left hand and pretend to be surprised that the rope has disappeared. Open your left hand wide, shake your head, and let your hand drop to your side. Turn your body toward the left and glance down at the floor, as though wondering if you might have dropped the rope.

As you turn your left side away from the audience for an instant, curl your left fingers up under the bottom edge of your jacket and pull the other ball of rope into your hand, closing your fingers around it. Don't move your arm—keep it at your side. Turn your body a little to the right, as you still look down at the floor as if searching for the vanished rope.

Then shrug and say, "Well, if I *did* have a rope, I would take it by the center. . . ," bringing your closed left fist up in front of you as if it were holding an imaginary rope by the center, ". . . and I would cut it in half so there would be two pieces." Clip the scissors together with your right fingers as if cutting a rope, and go through the rest of the motions.

"And then I would wrap it around my hand, say the magic words, and pull it out, fully restored and in one piece again." Reach into your left fist, grip the end of rope that sticks up out of the center of the ball, and pull the rope out of your fist, stretching it into view between your hands. "Hey, there it is! I knew I had a rope somewhere."

2

TRICKY KNOTS

BASIC TRICKY-KNOT ROUTINE

You can use rope, ribbon, or string for this do-anywhere routine of appearing and vanishing knots. It blends together seven of the standard tricky knots magicians have been using for years, in a sequence that quickly builds from one trick to the next, provides some amusing fun, and ends with a real puzzler.

The routine can be used by itself, as an introduction to rope tricks that are to follow, or it can be expanded by adding some of the other tricky knots explained elsewhere in this chapter.

How it looks

You take one end of a rope in your hand, hold it high, bring up the other end, and snap it out into the air. "This is an angry rope," you say. "It's fit to be *tied*." As you snap it into the air again, a knot suddenly appears, as if you had snapped the knot into the end of it!

Quickly untying the knot, you bring the two ends of the rope together, tie them, and tug at the ends to form a tight, hard knot. Holding up the loop to display the knot, you give the rope a quick shake. The knot vanishes and the ends fall apart, as you say, "But now the *tide* has gone out."

You take one end of the rope in each hand, stretching the rope between them. "This has been called the fastest knot in the world." Bringing your hands together for an instant, you pull them apart and an Overhand Knot appears at the center of the rope. "I'll do it again," you say, as you untie the knot and then seem to repeat exactly the same moves as before. But this time, you instantly produce a big Bow Knot and hold it up by its bows to show it, and quip, "My imitation of a giant tying his shoelace."

Shaking that knot from the rope, you tie another large Overhand Knot. The audience can see that it seems to be a genuine knot as you pull it tight. You drop one end of the rope to the floor and put your foot on it so that the rope, with the knot at the center, is stretched between hand and foot. When you snap your fingers, the knot instantly vanishes, and you say, "A little knot . . . that *is* not."

You drape the rope over the palm of your hand and lift it high, announcing, "One hand." With a quick twist and downward snap, you tie an instant One-Hand Knot.

After untying that knot, you say, "And now, here's how to tie a knot the hard way." You take one end of the rope in each hand. "If you want to have some fun when you go home, get a piece of rope such as this, or a piece of string, and try to tie a real knot in the center of it without letting go of either end . . . . It's supposed to be a physical impossibility."

You keep the ends of the rope in your hands, make some quick loops and twists, and stretch it out again between your hands to show a real knot tied at the center. "Well, they *say* it's impossible . . . Try it when you get home."

What you need

A 4½-foot length of soft white clothesline, or a similar length of string or satin ribbon.

The secret

The Snap Knot that starts the routine is really a trick rather than a tricky knot, since the knot that you seem to snap into the end of the rope has already been tied and is hidden in your hand until you switch the two rope ends. This is an ancient trick, but still a good one. Each of the other tricky knots will be explained in the order in which they are shown in the routine.

Prepare the rope by tying a large Overhand Knot (the everyday kind) about 4 inches from one end of it. Don't pull it tight; the knot should be only slightly smaller than the palm of your hand. Place the knot on the palm of your right hand, wind the rest of the rope loosely around the hand, and slip your hand out of it. Have the rope coiled that way in one of your right-hand pockets.

What you do

Put your right hand into your pocket, slide your fingers into the coil so the knot is against your palm, and bring the rope out with the back of your hand toward the audience. With your left hand, put the top end of the rope into the crotch of your right thumb to hold it so the secret knot is just beneath the thumb, hidden from front view by your hand. Uncoil the rest of the rope to let it hang down from your right hand.

The Snap Knot

Hold your right hand high to display the hanging rope. Grasp the bottom end of the rope with your left hand and bring that end up to hold it clipped between your right first and second fingers. Give your right hand a sharp downward shake and drop the end of the rope from between your fingers, as if snapping it down into the air to try to form a knot. When no knot appears the first time, you seem to do the same thing again. But what you really do the second time is switch the two ends.

Bring the hanging end up as before, with your left hand, and hold it clipped between your right fingers. Once more, give your right hand a sharp downward shake. But keep hold of the end that is between your fingers and just drop *the other end* from under

THE SNAP KNOT

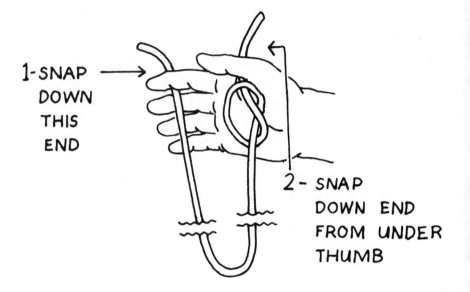

1-SNAP DOWN THIS END

2- SNAP DOWN END FROM UNDER THUMB

your thumb, so it snaps down and the hidden knot suddenly appears. Lift the rope to show the knot and then untie it.

Fake Square Knot

You now take an end of the rope in each hand and bring the two ends together just as if you were going to tie a real Square Knot. But instead of tying the first part of a real knot by *crossing* the ends under and over, you merely hold one end straight and twist the other end a full turn *around* it. Then you tie the second part of the knot exactly as you would tie the rest of a Square Knot, by crossing the ends over and under, and pulling them as tight as you can. The fake knot looks very real and will hold its shape until the rope is given a sharp downward shake to make the knot fall apart and disappear.

Here, in detail, is how to tie it:

With both palms up, hold the rope about 4 inches from each end, and bring your hands together. Lay the left end of the rope across the right end and hold both for a moment with the tip of the left thumb. With your right hand, turn the right end of the rope around the left end and out to the left. Again, hold both ends with the left thumb. Now, just tie the two ends together in a single knot.

With the lower fingers of each hand, grip the sides of the rope beneath the knot, and with your thumbs and first fingers pull hard on the rope ends to tighten the knot. Grasp the rope just above the knot with your right hand, remove your left hand, and display the tied-together loop. Give it a hard shake and the knot vanishes as the ends fall apart.

FAKE SQUARE KNOT

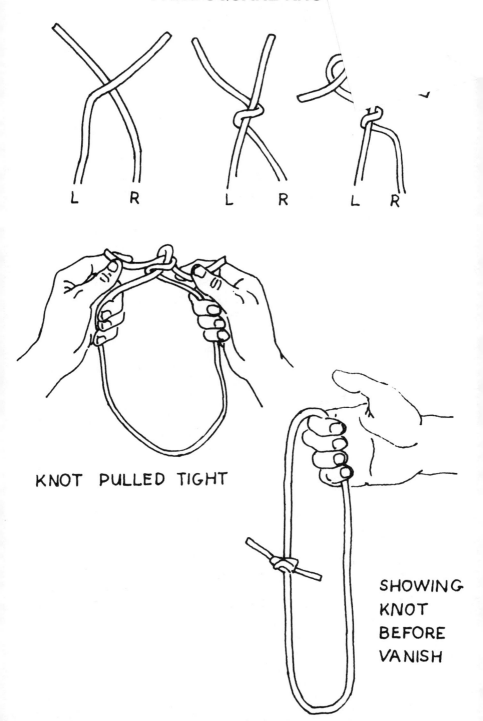

L   R   L   R   L   R

KNOT PULLED TIGHT

SHOWING
KNOT
BEFORE
VANISH

INSTANT KNOT

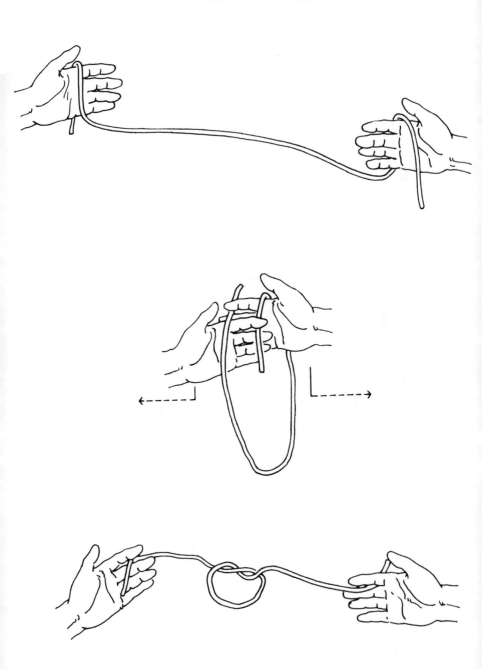

Instant Knot

This is the instant tying of an Overhand Knot as the rope is held out horizontally between your hands. With your left palm toward you, thumb up and fingertips to the right, drape one end of the rope over that hand so part of the end hangs down at the *back* of it. Take the other rope end in your right hand, but in the opposite way, so that end goes down across the *palm*. The right palm should be toward you, thumb up, and fingertips to the left. Hold the hands apart to show the rope hanging between them.

Bring your hands together, with the left hand nearest to your body, and touch the backs of the left fingertips against the palm of the right hand. This also puts the right fingertips at the back of the left hand. Tightly nip the *right* end of the rope between the *left* first and second fingers. At the same time, nip the *left* end between the *right* first and second fingers. Now, just pull your hands apart, straight out to the sides, and the Overhand Knot will form at the center of the rope.

This should all be done quickly, with your hands touching together for only an instant before they are drawn apart and the knot appears. After showing the knot, untie it.

INSTANT BOW KNOT

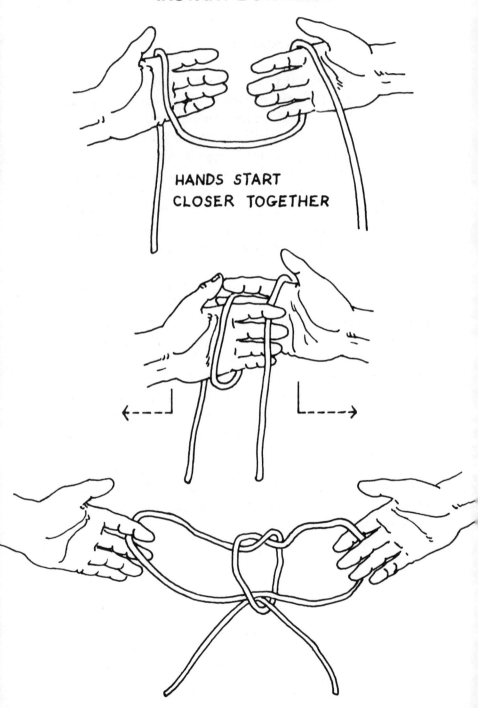

HANDS START
CLOSER TOGETHER

Instant Bow Knot

The instant tying of a Bow Knot is done the same way as the Overhand Knot, except that you start with your hands much closer together. Instead of holding the rope at the ends, hold it near the center so there is less than a foot of rope between your hands. The left side of the rope hangs down over the *back* of your left hand; the right side hangs down over the *palm* of your right hand.

Bring your hands together exactly as before. Grip the part of the rope that is in your *right* palm between the *left* first and second fingers. At the same time, grip the part at the back of the *left* hand between the *right* first and second fingers. Quickly draw your hands apart and you will be holding a large Bow Knot by its two big bows. (This happens because, with less rope between your hands, the two ends catch up into loops instead of passing through as when the single knot is formed.) Show the Bow Knot and then take one of the ends and shake the rope down so the knot unties.

Fake Overhand Knot

This closely imitates the tying of a genuine Overhand Knot, but one finger secretly holds back a tiny loop that converts it into a Slip Knot, which pulls apart and vanishes.

Hold your left palm toward you, back of the hand to the audience, thumb up, fingertips to the right. Hold the rope about a foot from one end and drape that part over the top edge of your left *second* finger near the tip, so the end passes between the first and second fingers and hangs down over the back of your hand. Loosely close your two lower left fingers over the part that passes down across the palm of the hand.

With your right hand, take the rope about a foot from the bottom end. Bring that end up across the other strand and under your left thumb to hold it, letting that end fall to the back of your left hand. Close your left second finger to press the tip of it against the point where the two strands cross in the form of an "X."

Reach out through the large loop with your right hand, take the end hanging at the back of the left fingers, and pull it in through the loop toward you, gradually forming a knot. As you continue to pull that end, a bight (loop) will catch around the tip of the left second finger. Slip this finger out of the bight as you finally draw the knot tight. The bight becomes caught in the tightening knot and makes it a Slip Knot.

Remove your right hand from the loop and hold the top rope end with your left hand so the rope hangs down to the floor. Step on the bottom end of

FAKE OVERHEAD KNOT

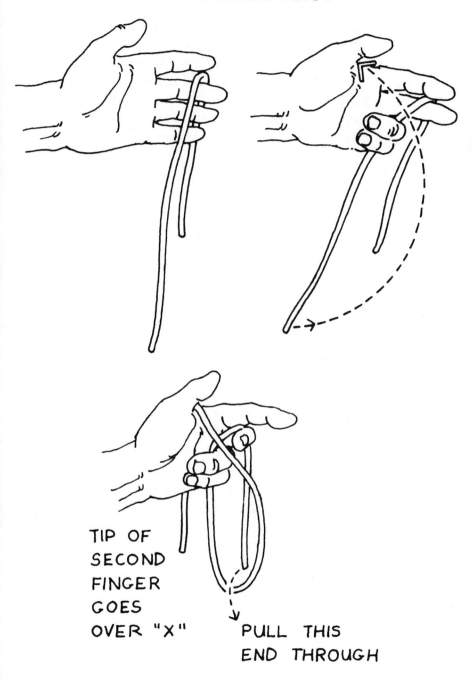

TIP OF
SECOND
FINGER
GOES
OVER "X"

PULL THIS
END THROUGH

the rope with your left foot and keep the rope tautly stretched between hand and foot. Point to the knot at the center with your right first finger. Pass your open right hand down in front of it and then quickly snap your right fingers and lift that hand away as you secretly pull upward on the rope with your left hand so the knot instantly vanishes.

Instant One-Hand Knot

Hold your right hand out to the right side, shoulder high and palm to the audience, thumb up and fingertips to the right. Lay the rope over the top edge of the right hand so that the part hanging down at the back of the hand is less than a foot long. Now, catch the longer part of the rope, which passes down across the palm, between the third and little fingers, and say, "One hand."

Bend the right hand straight down from the wrist, fingertips toward the floor and back under, and grasp the short end of the rope between the first and second fingers. Keep hold of that end and shake the loop down off the back of the hand, so it falls to form a knot on the hanging rope. With practice, this can be done so swiftly that the sudden appearance of the knot really looks like magic. Show the knot and untie it.

INSTANT ONE-HAND KNOT

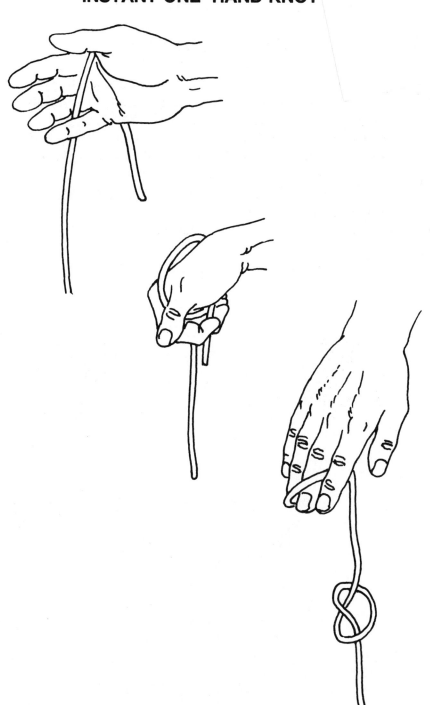

The Impossible Knot

It *would* be impossible to tie this knot at the center of the rope without letting go of either end, although that is what you seem to do. Secretly, you do release one of the ends, but in a way that brings that end back into your hand instantly and leaves the audience convinced that you never let go of it.

Take an end of the rope in each hand, thumbs up and palms toward you. Hold your hands apart so the rope's center hangs loosely between them. Without

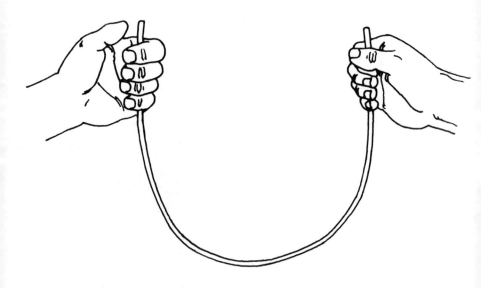

THE IMPOSSIBLE KNOT

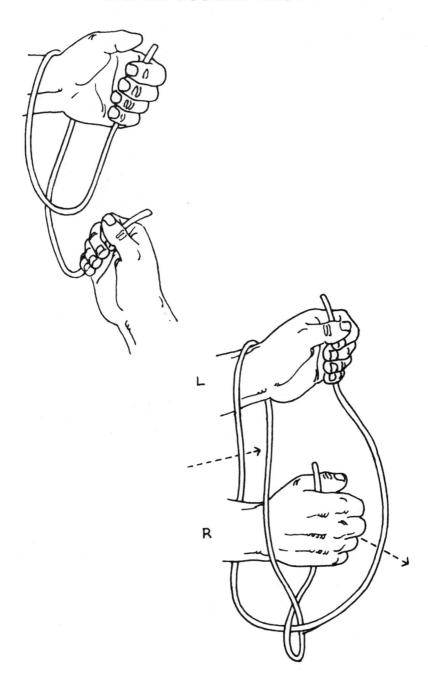

L

R

continued on next page . . .

THE IMPOSSIBLE KNOT—continued

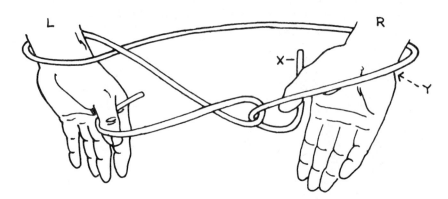

RIGHT THUMB RELEASES END "X" _
HAND CLOSES AROUND ROPE AT "Y"

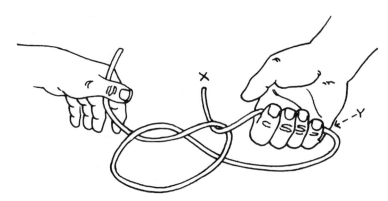

LOOPS DROP OFF BOTH HANDS

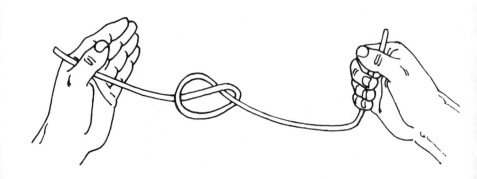

letting go of either end, bring your right hand up to the top of the left wrist and over the back of it to form a loop by draping the center of the rope over the top edge of the left wrist. Continue to draw your right hand down from the back of the left wrist until the right hand is about a foot beneath the bottom of the loop.

Lift your right hand toward you slightly and then push that hand *out from you* through the left side of the loop, to the *left* of the vertical strand that hangs down at the back of the loop. Twist the back of the right wrist out around that vertical strand, and then draw the right hand *in toward you* again, through the loop. Lift the right hand out to hold it in front of you, opposite the left hand.

At this point, a loop has been formed around each wrist, each hand still holds its end of the rope, and the knuckles of both hands are toward the front, thumbs up. The looped and twisted rope should be held tautly between them. You can pause, if you wish, to display the apparent knot that has been formed by the twisted loops. But from here on, the rest of the moves should be one continuous action, smoothly blended together without hesitation.

Turn both hands down toward the floor to let the loops fall off both wrists and, as you do that, secretly close the right fingers around the part of the rope that slides off the wrist into them, and release the end the right hand has been holding. As the loops fall, immediately draw both hands apart to tighten the knot that forms at the center of the rope, sliding your right hand out to its end, which seemingly has never left that hand. Hold up the rope, still gripped at both ends, and tell the audience, "Well, they say it's impossible ... Try it when you get home."

TWO MORE WITH ONE HAND

The Instant One-Hand Knot, previously explained in the *Basic Tricky-Knots Routine,* is among the showiest and most impressive of all knot flourishes. Here are two additional easy ways of performing it, both of which avoid the sometimes awkward positioning and wrist-twisting of the standard method.

Simplicity One-Hand Knot

How it looks

You hang the center of a rope over one hand, bring up the two ends, and hold them with the open palm of the hand toward the audience. Without any tricky moves, you simply drop one end and give the rope a sharp downward shake. A knot suddenly appears, tied at its center.

What you do

Hold your right hand with its palm toward you, thumb up, and fingertips to the left. Drape the center of the rope over the top of that hand, close to the thumb. Half the rope hangs down over the back of the hand and the other half hangs down over the palm.

Close your left hand into a loose fist around both hanging parts of the rope, slide the hand down to the

SIMPLICITY ONE-HAND KNOT

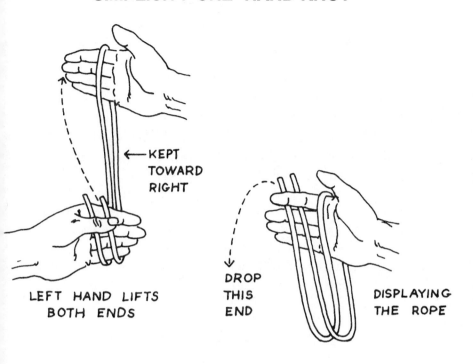

← KEPT
TOWARD
RIGHT

LEFT HAND LIFTS
BOTH ENDS

DROP
THIS
END

DISPLAYING
THE ROPE

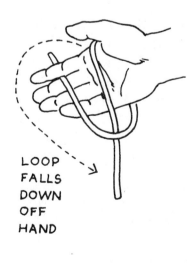

LOOP
FALLS
DOWN
OFF
HAND

bottom, lift both rope ends up together toward you, and bring the ends up to hold them between your right first and second fingers. (Be careful not to twist the ends as you lift them. The end that hangs down from the back of the right hand should be kept to the right.)

Turn the palm of your right hand to the audience to display the rope. When you are ready to produce the knot, drop the forward end of the rope from between your first and second fingers, keep hold of the other end, and in one continuing motion tilt your fingertips down toward the floor as you give your hand a sudden downward shake. The remaining loop will fall off your hand and form an instant knot at the rope's center.

Loop-Around One-Hand Knot

How it looks

Holding one end, you casually loop a rope around your hand, and turn the palm toward the audience so it can be seen that the rope is not twisted in any tricky way. Swinging the hand toward yourself again, you flick it down, and a knot instantly appears.

What you do

Start with the right palm toward you, thumb up, and fingertips to the left. Place one end of the rope into the crotch of the right thumb to hold it. Run your left hand down the rope to its center, bring that part up around the *back* of your right hand, and drape the center over the top edge of the right fin-

LOOP-AROUND ONE-HAND KNOT

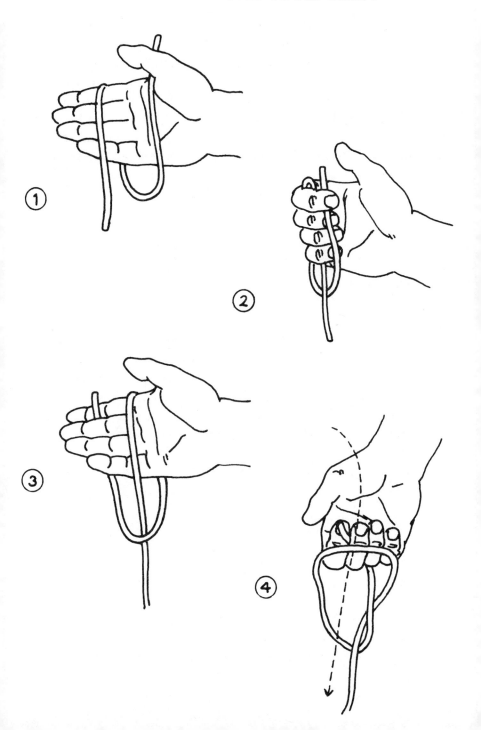

gers so the rope's other end hangs down across the palm. Remove your left hand.

Turn your right palm toward the audience to show the rope and then swing the palm toward you again. Quickly close your fingers against the palm, take the end of the rope out from under your thumb with your first and second fingers, and straighten out your hand. Tilt your fingertips toward the floor, give the hand a downward shake, and the knot appears at the center of the hanging rope.

A SPECTACLE OF KNOTS

How it looks

Here's a brief routine based on the tying of a single knot. You start by tying an ordinary Ring Hitch in the standard way, then demonstrate how it can be tied instantly with only one hand. Spreading out the knot's loops, you form them into an imitation pair of old-fashioned "spectacles." Finally, with a quick twisting of the loops, you magically transform the Hitch into two other knots that suddenly appear along the rope—an Overhand Knot and a Figure Eight.

What you need

A 4-foot length of soft clothesline.

What you do

To "set the stage" for the instant one-hand tying that is to come, you first tie a Ring Hitch with both hands, as follows. Take the rope at its center with your right hand and turn the left palm toward you. Place the center loop under the left thumb to hold it there, with about 2 inches of the loop extending above your left hand. Grasp both bottom ends of the rope with your right hand and bring them up together in front of the palm, over the left thumb, and through the center loop. Pull them down to form the ordinary Ring Hitch around the left thumb and turn the hand palm-outward to display it.

"This knot has a dozen different names and a hundred different uses," you say. "It is called a Cow Hitch, a Carriage Hitch, a Sling Hitch, a Hoist Hitch, a Ring Hitch, and most of us know it as a Tag Knot, used for tying price tags to things."

The One-Hand Ring Hitch

As you speak, untie the Hitch from your left thumb by pulling out the two ends, and take the center of the rope with your left hand. Hold out your right hand with its palm toward the floor, fingertips toward the right, and the tip of the thumb thrust straight out toward the audience. Drape the center of the rope over the right thumb, so both ends hang down evenly at the bottom.

"Sailors sometimes called it a Lanyard Hitch," you say, "and some old salts could tie it quicker than you can blink . . . and with only one hand."

Bend your right fingers down and back toward you to grasp between the first and second fingers the part of the rope that hangs nearest to your body. Twist your hand toward the rear and then up and straight out to the right again, palm down as at the start. This catches a little loop around the tip of the

ONE-HAND RING HITCH

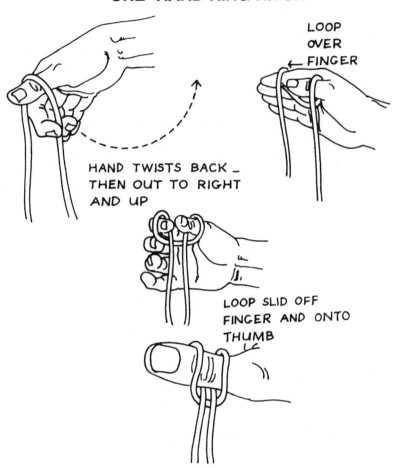

LOOP
OVER
FINGER

HAND TWISTS BACK _
THEN OUT TO RIGHT
AND UP

LOOP SLID OFF
FINGER AND ONTO
THUMB

A PAIR OF SPECTACLES

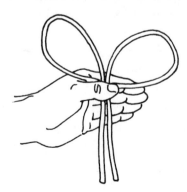

TWO KNOTS FROM ONE

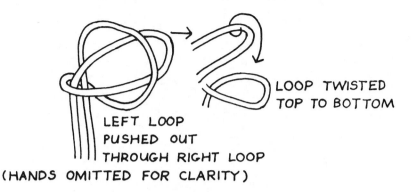

LOOP TWISTED
TOP TO BOTTOM

LEFT LOOP
PUSHED OUT
THROUGH RIGHT LOOP

(HANDS OMITTED FOR CLARITY)

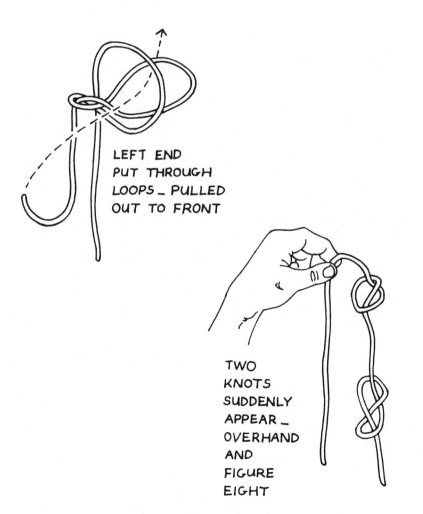

LEFT END
PUT THROUGH
LOOPS — PULLED
OUT TO FRONT

TWO
KNOTS
SUDDENLY
APPEAR —
OVERHAND
AND
FIGURE
EIGHT

first finger. Without pausing, turn the hand thumb-upward, palm toward the audience, and press the tip of the first finger against the tip of the thumb. Slide the loop off the finger and on to the thumb to complete the instant One-Hand Ring Hitch, timing the movements of your hand to the words as you say, "Just . . . like . . . this!"

A Pair of Spectacles

Hold your right hand high to show the Hitch tied around your thumb, then bring that hand down in front of you, palm toward you. Bring your left hand, palm toward you, over beneath the right thumb, and slide the bottom of the loop down about 2 inches. Grip it there, along with the two hanging strands, between your left thumb and first finger, and slide the Hitch off your right thumb. (Your left hand will hold the rope as it is until the end of the routine.) With your right hand, turn the two side loops of the Hitch out flat to the left and right and shape them with your fingers to look like a pair of large eyeglasses. Turn your left palm out to show the "glasses" and say, "A pair of old-fashioned spectacles." Lift them to your eyes and look out at the audience through them. "*Spectacular*—isn't it?"

Two Knots from One

Bring your left hand down in front of you, turning the palm toward you again. With your right hand, bend the left loop over to the right, push it out through the right loop from back to front, and then give it one quick downward twist from top to bottom, moving your left thumb a little to take a fresh grip on the two loops at their base.

"We had one knot," you say, as you reach down with your right hand to take the end of the rope that is hanging to the *left* and hold it up. "But if this goes into that ... " Push that end of the rope through both loops at once, from back to front, and draw the end out to the front as you release the loops from under your left thumb to hold the rope stretched between your hands. Two knots suddenly appear, spaced along the rope — "... now we have two, a pair of knots everybody knows."

Drop the end of the rope from your right hand, hold the dangling rope high with your left hand, and point with your right finger to one knot and then the other. "An Overhand Knot and a Figure Eight."

KNOT A ROPE AND CATCH A RIBBON

How it looks

You show a rope, tie it into a large loop and, as you pull your hands apart and tighten the knot, a bright red ribbon suddenly appears, tied to the center of the rope.

What you need

A 4-foot length of soft white clothesline.
A 3-foot length of red satin ribbon, 1 inch wide.
A wire twist-tie, the kind made for tying plastic sandwich bags.

The secret

The ribbon, tightly rolled into a small coil around the rope, is secretly hidden in one hand from the time the rope is first shown. But the rope is so freely displayed and drawn back and forth through the hand that the sudden appearance of the ribbon tied to the rope takes the audience by surprise.

Lay the ribbon out horizontally flat on a table top. Place the center of the rope vertically on top of the center of the horizontal ribbon. Fold the left side of the ribbon over to bring both ends together at the right, so the ribbon is now at a right angle to the rope.

Take both ends of the ribbon together and start rolling the doubled ribbon tightly in upon itself toward the center of the rope, continuing until the entire ribbon has been rolled up beside the rope.

Wrap the twist-tie tightly around the rope and ribbon to hold them together. The twist-tie is used simply to keep the rolled ribbon securely in place, so you can prepare the rope in advance and carry it with the rest of your props. The final set-up, done just before your performance, takes only a second. Place the rope on the table with its center hidden behind some other prop, and then unfasten the twist-tie and discard it, leaving the coiled ribbon lying beside the rope's center and to its right.

What you do

Take up the rope at its center with your right hand, by closing your fingers into a loose fist around both the rope and ribbon. Turn the back of your hand toward the audience and lift up the rope to show it, keeping the ribbon hidden inside your fingers.

With your left hand, take the end of the rope that hangs down nearest you. Draw that end down, pulling the rope down through your right fist and the concealed ribbon until only about 3 inches of rope extend above the top of the right hand. Then, lift your left hand, with the end of rope it is holding, up opposite your right hand. At this point, each hand should be holding one end of the rope in a similar way, fingers closed around it and backs of the hands toward the audience. Pause a moment to display the plain rope hanging down between your hands.

Bring your left hand over to your right hand, and lay the left end of the rope across the right end to tie a knot that forms a big loop. Then, take both rope ends and hold them with the left hand. Without opening the right hand, slide it and the hidden ribbon down the rope to its center at the bottom of the loop.

Immediately, raise the right hand up again, lifting the center part of the rope that your hand is still closed around. Quickly take the right end of the rope away from your left hand, by gripping that end between your right thumb and first finger. Keep the other rope end in your left hand and suddenly pull both hands wide apart and out to the sides, finally opening your right fist to release the ribbon.

The outward pull of your hands jerks the suddenly unrolling ribbon into view and tightens the knot around it as it magically appears, tied at the center of the rope.

KNOT A ROPE AND CATCH A RIBBON

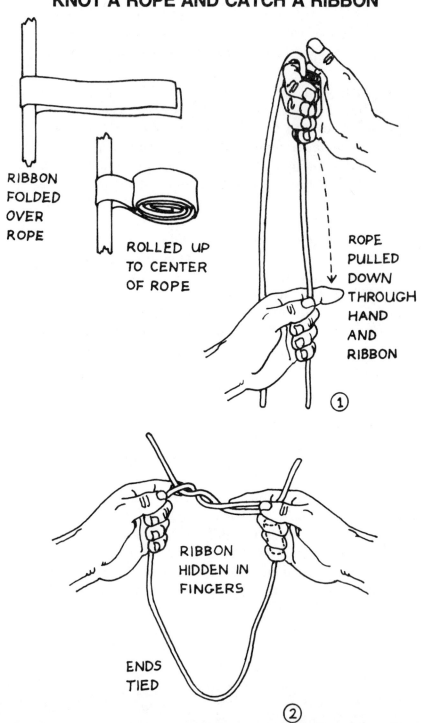

RIBBON
FOLDED
OVER
ROPE

ROLLED UP
TO CENTER
OF ROPE

ROPE
PULLED
DOWN
THROUGH
HAND
AND
RIBBON

①

RIBBON
HIDDEN IN
FINGERS

ENDS
TIED

②

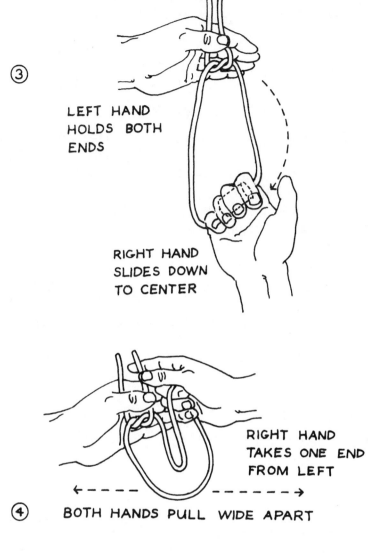

③

LEFT HAND
HOLDS BOTH
ENDS

RIGHT HAND
SLIDES DOWN
TO CENTER

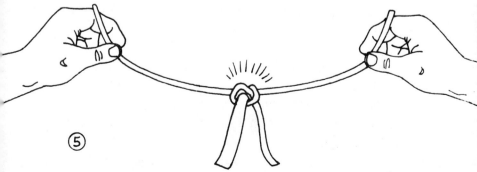

RIGHT HAND
TAKES ONE END
FROM LEFT

④ BOTH HANDS PULL WIDE APART

⑤

TRIPLE FLYING KNOTS

How it looks

"One knot ... Two knots ... Three knots," you say, as you tie three knots, spaced along a length of rope. Holding one rope end in each hand, you suddenly snap the center of the rope forward, as if throwing the knots out into the audience. All three knots vanish. "There they go! ... Knots to you!"

Quickly you coil up the rope, take it by one end, and hold it high."Now watch them all fly back again. ... Knots to me!" You give the rope a sharp shake and, as it uncoils, three knots appear once more, spaced down along it. Pointing to each knot, you count them aloud, "One ... Two ... Three!"

What you need

A 4-foot length of soft clothesline.
Double-faced transparent tape, the kind that is sticky on both sides.

The secret

The rope has bands of the double-faced tape spaced along it, which help you to tie a row of three fake knots. The knots look genuine, but they instantly fall apart and vanish when the ends of the rope are pulled. The way the rope is then coiled around the hand secretly forms the three knots that "fly back again."

To prepare the rope, start 6 inches in from one end and wrap a 2-inch length of the double-faced

tape in a *tight* band around it. Move along the rope 6
inches and wrap another strip of tape tightly around
it. Continue until you have wrapped six little strips
of sticky tape around the rope, spaced 6 inches apart.
(After the rope has been used a dozen or so times,
the tape should be snipped off and replaced with new
pieces.)

What you do

Pick up the rope and hold it with both hands
about a foot in from the left end. The hands should
be palms down, with the rope held between the
thumb and first two fingers of each hand. Casually
slide your hands a little apart along the rope until
you feel the first two sticky bands of tape with your
left and right fingers.

Holding those two bands, move your right hand
forward toward the audience and then over to the
left to form a loop in the rope that brings the two
sticky tapes together. Give them a little squeeze
with your left thumb and finger so they stick together tightly.

Keep that loop held as it is with your left hand.
Slide your right hand loosely along the whole length
of the rope to its right end. Take that end and put it
in through the loop *from the front*, pointing the end
toward yourself. Draw the end through, just as if tying a knot, then drop that end and bring your right
hand back to hold the rope near its center. Remove
your left hand and let the first knot dangle down.

Repeat the same moves to tie a second false knot
with the second set of sticky tapes, and then a third
knot with the third pair of tapes.

Hold one rope end in each hand, with the rope

hanging somewhat slackly between them, and display the row of knots. Swing the center of the rope forward, as if "throwing" the knots, and suddenly stretch both hands out to the sides to snap the rope taut. That pulls the stuck-together loops apart and all three knots instantly vanish.

Drop the left end of the rope from the left hand and turn the palm of this hand toward you. Bring the right rope end over and put that end into the crotch of the left thumb, closing the thumb to hold it there. Remove your right hand so the rope is left hanging down from your left hand.

What you seem to do now is to gather up the rope in a series of loops quickly and casually, hanging each of the loops over your left hand to coil the rope around it. But this looping is done in a way that secretly forms three knots that will appear when the rope is shaken out.

Bring your right hand, palm up, under the rope that hangs down from your left hand, so the rope lies across both palms and so the little fingers of both hands are about 6 inches apart. The right side of the rope should pass under the right thumb.

Close the right fingers to make a fist, and then turn your right hand counterclockwise, palm downward. A loop of rope now runs through your right fingers. Hang that loop over the outstretched fingers of your left hand and leave it there.

Turn the right palm up again and move it along the rope to where you can make a second loop the same way. Hang that loop over your left hand. Then, make a similar third loop and hang it over your left hand.

Now, put the first two fingers of your right hand

TRIPLE FLYING KNOTS—1

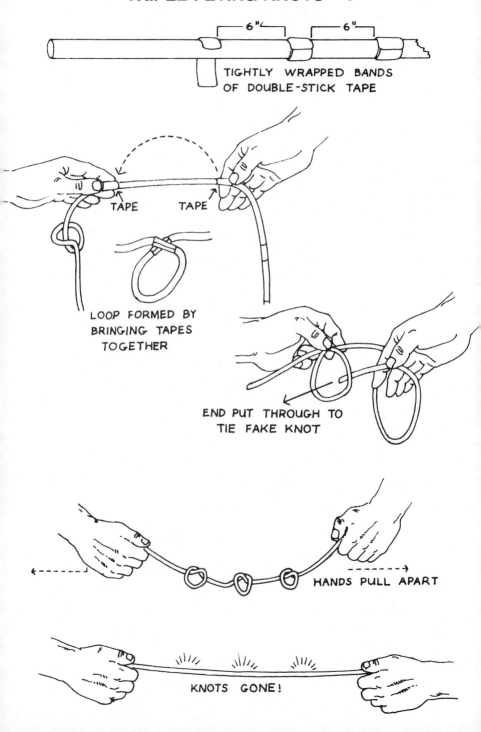

TIGHTLY WRAPPED BANDS OF DOUBLE-STICK TAPE

TAPE TAPE

LOOP FORMED BY BRINGING TAPES TOGETHER

END PUT THROUGH TO TIE FAKE KNOT

HANDS PULL APART

KNOTS GONE!

TRIPLE FLYING KNOTS—2

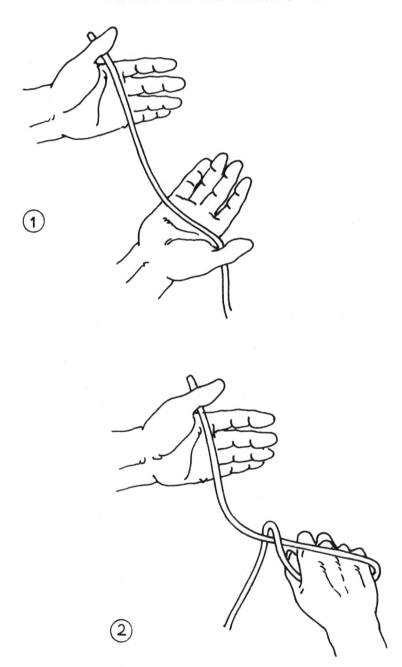

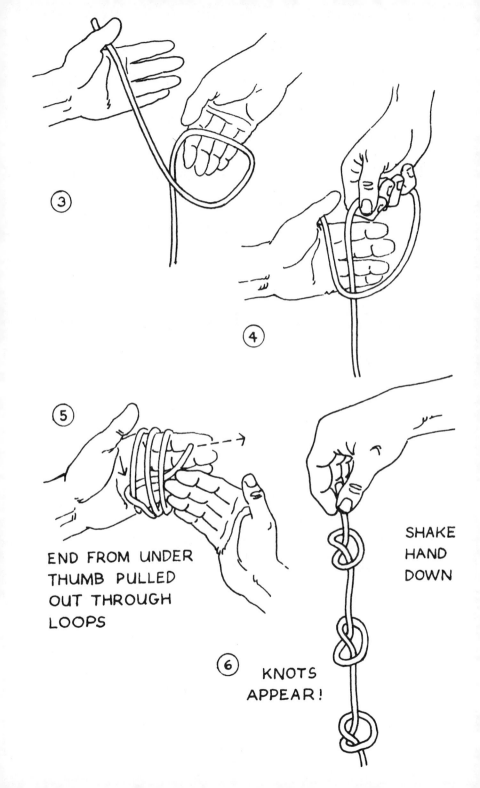

③

④

⑤

END FROM UNDER
THUMB PULLED
OUT THROUGH
LOOPS

⑥ KNOTS
APPEAR!

SHAKE
HAND
DOWN

in *through* all the loops that hang over your left hand. With those fingers, grip the end of the rope held under your left thumb. Pull that end out to the right, up through the coils.

Slide the coiled rope off your left hand, grasp the end with your right hand, and hold the rope up high, still coiled as it hangs from your hand. Give it a sharp downward shake and, as it comes uncoiled, the three knots will appear, spaced down along it.

3

PENETRATIONS

COFFEE, TEA, OR MAGIC

How it looks

You show a rope and drape the center of it over
your hand so the two ends hang to the bottom. Then,
you pick up a coffee cup and hold it by its handle
with the same hand. "I call this one 'Coffee, Tea, or
Magic,'" you say. "I'm sorry there is no coffee or tea
to offer you. But there is—*magic*!"

You grip the cup with your other hand and
quickly pull it down to leave it hanging at the center

COFFEE, TEA, OR MAGIC

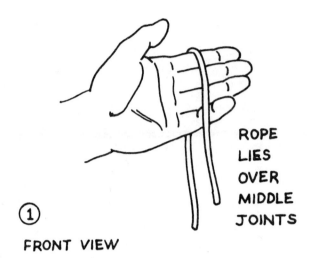

ROPE
LIES
OVER
MIDDLE
JOINTS

① FRONT VIEW

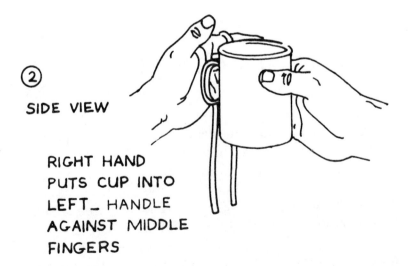

② SIDE VIEW

RIGHT HAND
PUTS CUP INTO
LEFT_ HANDLE
AGAINST MIDDLE
FINGERS

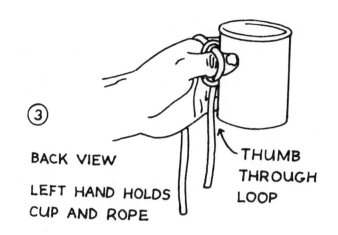

③

BACK VIEW

LEFT HAND HOLDS
CUP AND ROPE

THUMB
THROUGH
LOOP

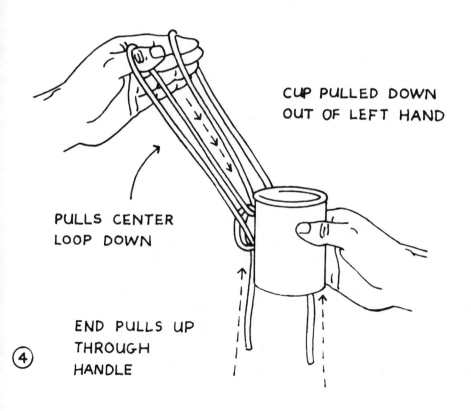

CUP PULLED DOWN
OUT OF LEFT HAND

PULLS CENTER
LOOP DOWN

END PULLS UP
THROUGH
HANDLE

④

of the rope, magically linked to the rope by its handle. Taking one end of the rope in each hand, you tilt the rope up and down so the linked cup slides back and forth on it. "At least, it's a new way to dry the dishes," you say. "Just hang them out on the line."

What you need

> A 3-foot length of soft clothesline.
> A coffee mug with a large handle.

The secret

As you place the cup in your hand at the start of the trick, you secretly push a small loop through the handle and hook it over the tip of the thumb holding the cup. When you pull the cup down, it automatically draws one of the rope's ends through the handle, but it happens so quickly spectators will be convinced the two ends were never out of sight.

There is nothing to prepare. Just have the cup and rope on your table.

What you do

Show the rope and hold it at the center with your right hand, so the two ends hang down. Hold your left hand out to the side of your body, fingertips to the left and palm toward the audience. Hang the center of the rope over the top of the left fingers, with the part that comes down the front of the hand lying against the fingers' middle joints.

Pick up the cup by holding the front of it, leaving the handle free, and bring it to the held-out left hand. As your hands come together, the cup and right hand partly hide the left hand from front view, which covers the one secret move you have to make. There's no need to hurry, but it should look as though you are merely taking the cup from your right hand with the left. Here, in detail, is what you do:

With your right hand, touch the back of the cup's handle against the two middle left fingers close to where they join the palm. Draw back the left second finger and with the tip of it push a little loop of rope through the handle toward you. Stick your left thumb up through that loop and hook it well over the tip of the thumb. Then, close the left thumb and fingers against the sides of the handle to hold the cup and remove your right hand.

Holding your fingers that way, you can show the cup and rope quite freely, since the secret loop is hidden behind the cup. Now, turn your left hand in toward you, with its back to the audience, and hold it high in front of you. When you are ready to link the cup to the rope, grasp the cup firmly with your right hand around the outside of it, fingers in front and thumb at the back.

Quickly pull the cup straight down toward the floor, closing your left hand around the two ends of the rope to hold them as they are drawn to the top of the hand and the center loop is pulled to the bottom. Swiftly pulling the cup down automatically draws the rope through the cup's handle.

Remove your right hand and leave the cup hanging at the bottom of the loop. Then bring the right hand up, take one end of the rope from your left hand, and spread your hands apart. Tilt your hands up and down so the cup slides back and forth on the rope stretched between them.

AT THE SPECTATOR'S COMMAND

How it looks

You thread a ribbon through a large brass ring, tie the ends of the ribbon so the ring hangs at the bottom of the knotted loop, and thread six smaller brass rings on the ribbon. Holding an empty paper bag open end downward with your other hand, you put the ribbon and rings up into the bag, pull the top end of the ribbon up through a slit in the bag, and hang that end over your finger so it remains in full view.

"Unless there is some magic that can pass solid metal through solid metal, there is no way the rings can be removed from the ribbon," you say, as you shake the upside-down bag to rattle the rings held on the ribbon inside it. You turn to one of the spectators. "Will you, sir, please command the magic to happen? Whenever you wish, just shout out the word 'Now!'"

The instant he shouts, the six small rings fall free, dropping from the paper bag to clatter on the table. You pull the ribbon up through the slit in the bag to show that the big ring still hangs at the bottom of the knotted loop. The other rings seem to have passed right through it at the spectator's command.

What you need

A 19-inch length of bright red satin ribbon, 1 inch wide.

A thick brass-plated metal ring about 3 inches in diameter.

Six smaller brass-plated rings, each about 1¼ inches in diameter. (Such rings are available in various sizes at sewing and needlework counters and at craft and hobby shops.)

A flat-bottomed brown paper "lunch" bag, approximately 10 inches high and 5 inches wide.

A pair of scissors.

The secret

The two ends of the loop are secretly switched when the ribbon is put up into the bag at the start of the trick. It is really the bottom end of the ribbon that is pulled up through the slit, instead of the ribbon's top end as the audience believes. Part of the ribbon is held pinched inside a corner of the bag by your fingers, holding the bag from the outside, which is what keeps the rings from falling off the ribbon until the spectator gives his command.

Open the paper bag, turn it bottom up, and use the scissors to cut a horizontal slit across the bottom to within ½ inch of each side. That is the only preparation. The props are not faked in any way. Have the opened bag on your table with its *bottom toward the audience* and the rings and ribbon beside it. (The bag is placed that way so you can pick it up to hold it at the corner where your fingers will need to be to hold the ribbon.)

What you do

Show the large ring and ribbon, thread the ring on the ribbon, and bring the two ribbon ends to the

AT THE SPECTATOR'S COMMAND

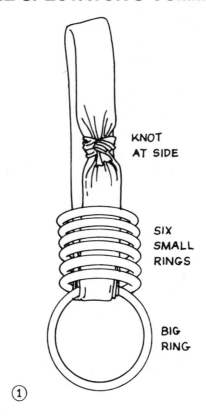

KNOT
AT SIDE

SIX
SMALL
RINGS

BIG
RING

①

②

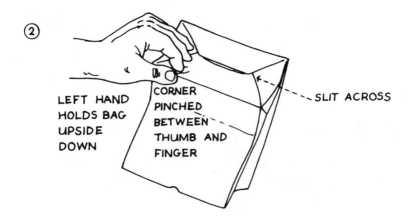

LEFT HAND
HOLDS BAG
UPSIDE
DOWN

CORNER
PINCHED
BETWEEN
THUMB AND
FINGER

- - - SLIT ACROSS

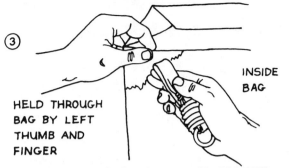

③ HELD THROUGH
BAG BY LEFT
THUMB AND
FINGER

INSIDE
BAG

TOP OF LOOP PUT UP INTO CORNER

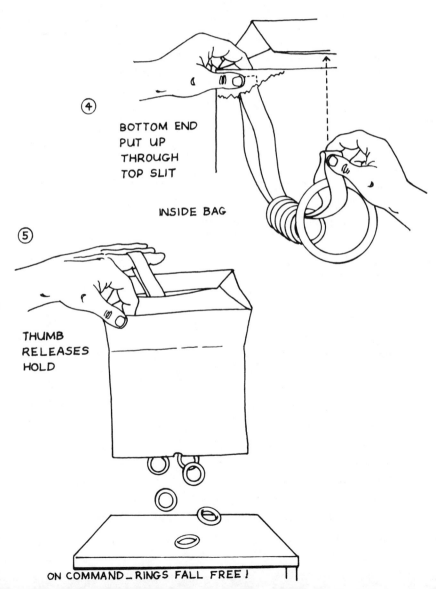

④ BOTTOM END
PUT UP
THROUGH
TOP SLIT

INSIDE BAG

⑤ THUMB
RELEASES
HOLD

ON COMMAND — RINGS FALL FREE!

top so the ring hangs at the bottom. Hold the ends together and tie them with a small single knot. Show the knot by drawing the ribbon out a little to the right, so that the knot will be at the right-hand side of the loop, *not* at the top.

Take the small rings, one at a time, and thread them down over the ribbon to the big ring at the bottom. Then hold the ribbon loop about an inch from the top between your right thumb and first finger. Pick up the paper bag with the left hand by bringing the palm of that hand against the bottom of the bag at its upper left corner, so that you can hold it at that corner between the left thumb and first finger. Hold the bag open end downward.

With your right hand, bring the ribbon up inside the bag to the left corner. Pinch that corner of the bag from the outside between your left thumb and finger to hold the top end of the ribbon. Grip it tightly through the bag. Immediately move your right hand down a little inside the bag and pinch the *bottom* end of the loop, the part of the ribbon that lies over the big ring, between your right thumb and first finger. Pull that end straight up and push it out through the slit in the bag so you can hang that loop over your extended left second finger. Lift that finger so the audience can see the loop hanging there, and remove your right hand from the bag.

To the audience, this should look as if you merely brought the top end of the ribbon up through the bag and out the slit. But the ends have now been switched to turn the ribbon loop upside down. The small rings would fall right off it except for the fact that what was the top end is now secretly held inside the corner of the bag, gripped there by the pressure of your left thumb and finger from the outside.

Hold the bag that way with your left hand and rattle the rings inside it. Bring the open end of the bag down close to the top of the table, and tell the spectator, "Whenever you wish, just shout out the word 'Now!' "

When he calls his command, lift your left thumb slightly to release that end of the ribbon. The rings fall down and out of the bag to clatter to the table. With your right hand, pull the entire ribbon up through the slit in the bag and hold it high to show that the big ring still hangs at the bottom of it.

OFF-AGAIN, ON-AGAIN RING AND STRING

How it looks

You give someone a small plastic ring to hold for a moment while you show a string and bring its two ends together in your left hand so it forms a loop with its center at the bottom. Taking the ring, you thread it on the string and knot the ends of the string together. The ring hangs at the bottom of the loop.

Reaching down with your right hand, you magically pull the ring right through the string, and it visibly comes off into your hand. Then, you put the ring into the hand holding the string, pull it down along the string again, and the two become linked. The ring is back on the tied loop of string, and the ring and string can be thoroughly examined.

What you need

A 3½-foot length of string.
Two identical plastic curtain rings, ¾ inch in diameter.
A facial tissue.
A coping saw or other small handsaw for cutting thin plastic.

The secret

Although the audience is aware of only one ring, two rings are used, one of them faked by being cut. The fake is made by simply clamping one of the rings upright and sawing straight down through one side. Because of the springy plastic, the cut ends hold together, leaving a small slit that can be pushed open to pass the string through it. The rings are handled so that nobody gets a close look at the cut one.

Thread the faked ring on the string and bring it to the center, with both ends of the string hanging down from the ring. Loosely gather up the string and put it into the left pocket of your jacket so that the threaded ring lies on top of the bunched string. Crumple the facial tissue and stuff it down inside your breast pocket to slightly bulge open the top of that pocket. Have the unfaked ring in your right pocket.

What you do

Take out the unfaked ring, show it, and say, "This ring has a hole in it." Give it to someone and ask, "Can you find the hole?" While he is examining it, reach into your left pocket with the left hand. Get the edge of the faked ring into the crotch between your first and second fingers, so you can hold it between the sides of those fingers at their base, and then bring out the bunched string with the back of that hand toward the audience.

Shake out the string so both ends hang down. Take the end that is toward you, bring it up to the top, and drop it down over the back of your left hand. You can now draw the string back and forth through your hand and through the ring that is secretly threaded on it, and it looks to the audience as if you were merely holding a length of string.

Draw the string down until about 3 inches extend above the top of the left hand. Bring the bottom end up and hold both ends beside each other at the top, forming a loop with its center hanging at the bottom.

Ask the person who is examining the ring, "Did you find the hole?" Then smile, and explain, "The hole in the ring is the part in the center—like the hole in a doughnut." (This little joke provides a way to have the ring examined and also lets you take your time getting the string and faked ring out of your pocket and positioned properly.)

Take the unfaked ring from the spectator. Hold it by one side between your right thumb and first finger and thread it over the top left end of the string. Bring it down inside your left hand until that ring rests on top of the split ring hidden there. Press your left thumb against both rings to hold them together and remove your right hand for an instant. Then, bring your right hand up inside your left hand again. Draw the bottom ring (the split one) down the string to the bottom of the loop and leave it hanging

OFF–AGAIN ON–AGAIN RING AND STRING

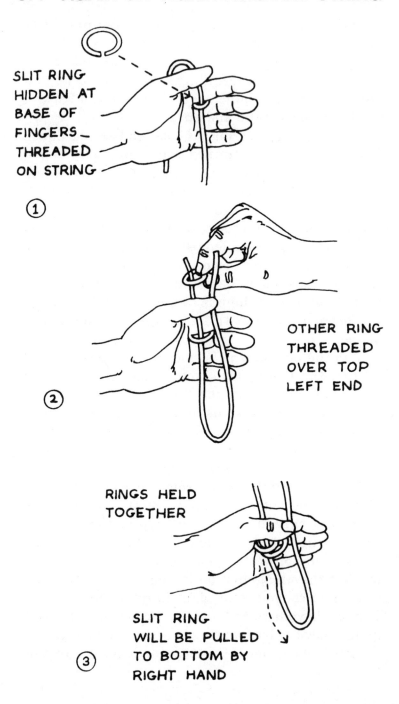

SLIT RING
HIDDEN AT
BASE OF
FINGERS—
THREADED
ON STRING

①

OTHER RING
THREADED
OVER TOP
LEFT END

②

RINGS HELD
TOGETHER

SLIT RING
WILL BE PULLED
TO BOTTOM BY
RIGHT HAND

③

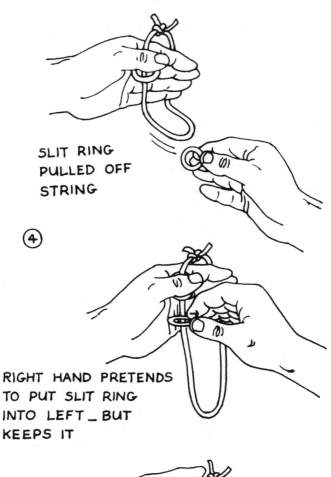

SLIT RING
PULLED OFF
STRING

④

RIGHT HAND PRETENDS
TO PUT SLIT RING
INTO LEFT _ BUT
KEEPS IT

⑤

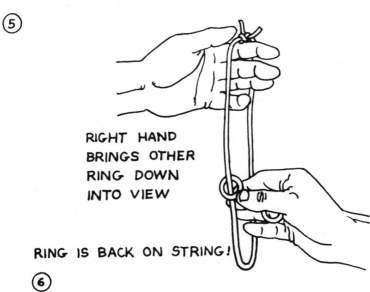

RIGHT HAND
BRINGS OTHER
RING DOWN
INTO VIEW

RING IS BACK ON STRING!

⑥

there. Your left thumb keeps the other ring pressed against the inside of the fingers.

Use both hands to tie the top ends of the string together, keeping the lower fingers partly closed so the left hand can hide its ring during the tying. Draw the knot out a little between your hands to show it, and then remove your right hand, keeping the string held up with your left hand.

Bring your right hand down to the split ring that now hangs at the bottom of the loop. Take the ring in that hand, feeling around it with the thumb to find the split. Secretly push it open and pull the ring right off the string. Show the ring with your right hand, holding it up between the thumb and first two fingers, with the tip of the thumb covering the split.

Now, bring your right hand up to your left, as if to put the ring into the left hand to leave it there. But as your hands come together, simply push the front edge of that ring against the inside of your left hand, so the ring is pushed back into your right fingers where your thumb can hold it. Keep the fake ring in the right hand. With the tips of your right fingers, pull the other ring (the unfaked one) straight down along the string out of your left hand. They appear linked again, with the ring back on the string, hanging at the bottom.

Keep the backs of your right fingers toward the audience and bring the right hand up near the top of the loop. With that hand, take one strand of the string and draw the hand straight back toward your body. At the same time, move your left hand straight out to the front, holding the loop between your two hands. This brings your right hand directly above your bulged-open breast pocket. Let the split ring secretly drop from your right hand into that pocket and immediately swing both hands out horizontally in front of you, tilting the loop up and down to slide the other ring back and forth on it.

You are now "clean," with nothing to hide, as you hand the knotted string and the ring to the spectator, and say, "I told you there was a hole in the ring—but that has nothing to do with the magic."

DISCO MAGIC

How it looks

"Here's something you can do with old records when you're tired of playing them," you say, as you show two phonograph records and a red ribbon. You thread the ribbon through the hole in one of the records, tie it around, and then hang the other record on the ribbon. "Just string them up like this, hang them from the ceiling, and you've got yourself a work of art—a disco mobile! It's practically priceless. *Nobody* would pay *any* price to have it."

You take one end of the ribbon in each hand, so the records hang fastened at its center. "I could tell you that this mobile is an artistic expression of the Thirteenth Dimension," you say. "But you wouldn't know what I was talking about—and neither would I. All I know is that if you watch it long enough, you get the sensation that these records melt right through the ribbon and flip themselves off into space. Of course, it doesn't really happen. But it sure *looks* like it happens."

As you draw your hands apart, the two records

pop up into the air and fall free, seeming to visibly penetrate the ribbon. "There they go!"

What you need

A 42-inch length of red satin ribbon, 1 inch wide. Two standard 45 RPM phonograph records. These have center holes about 1½ inches in diameter. (Choose records you no longer want to play, because using them in the trick will scratch them.)

The secret

The records and ribbon are unprepared and nothing else is used. The whole secret is in the handling of the ribbon, which involves an easy and convincing switch of the two ends. Have the records and ribbon on your table.

What you do

Hold one of the records upright with your left hand by placing that hand around the left side of the record near the top, fingers in front, and thumb at the rear. Hang the center of the ribbon over the top edge of the record, then pull the ribbon at the back down a few inches so the front end is a little shorter than the back end.

Place the tip of your left thumb on the left edge of the ribbon that hangs down at the back. Your thumb should be just above and slightly to the left of the record's center hole. Keep the left edge of the ribbon held under your thumb during the moves that follow.

What you *seem* to do now, as the audience sees

it, is to bring the front end of the ribbon in through the hole in the record, then up over the top, and back down through the hole again. But what you *really* do is switch the two ends of the ribbon. The switch is almost automatic.

Start with your right hand at the front of the record. Push part of the ribbon in through the center hole from the front, so that a small loop hangs through toward the back. Move your right hand to the back with its palm toward you. Put your first finger through the ribbon loop, and then bring the rest of the fingers beneath the ribbon that hangs down over the back of the record.

Now, simply slide your right hand straight down the ribbon to the very bottom end. This pulls the rest of the front end of the ribbon in through the hole. But since that end was shorter, moving your hand down also pulls the short *front* end out of your fingers and leaves them holding the bottom end of the *back* part of the ribbon. (This has been explained in detail so you will understand what happens, but you don't have to think about it while performing the trick. Just bring your hand straight down along the ribbons and the switch is automatic.)

Without pausing, lift the bottom ribbon end right up over the top edge of the record, down the front to the center hole, then push that end through the hole, front to back.

The edge of ribbon your left thumb has been holding since the start of the trick will be twisted into a loop by this switching of the ribbon's ends. That loop, hidden at the back behind the top of the record, is the real center of the ribbon. Hold that loop firmly with your left thumb. Bring your right hand down to the two bottom ends of the ribbon and

DISCO MAGIC

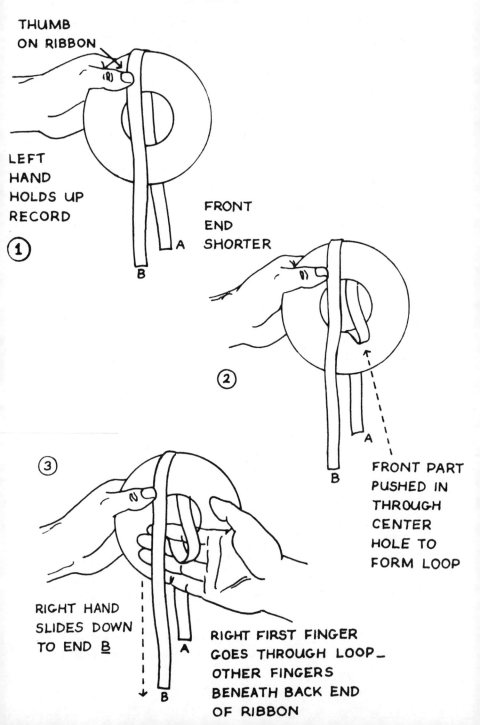

THUMB
ON RIBBON

LEFT
HAND
HOLDS UP
RECORD

①

FRONT
END
SHORTER

A

B

②

FRONT PART
PUSHED IN
THROUGH
CENTER
HOLE TO
FORM LOOP

A

B

③

RIGHT HAND
SLIDES DOWN
TO END B

RIGHT FIRST FINGER
GOES THROUGH LOOP—
OTHER FINGERS
BENEATH BACK END
OF RIBBON

A

B

TOP OF OTHER RECORD
WILL GO HERE

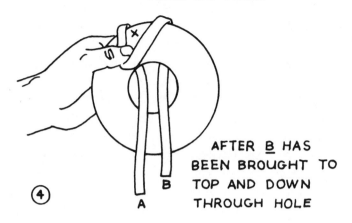

④

AFTER B HAS
BEEN BROUGHT TO
TOP AND DOWN
THROUGH HOLE

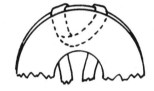

⑤

LOOP SANDWICHED BETWEEN
TOP EDGES OF RECORDS

BOTH RECORDS
HANG ON RIBBON

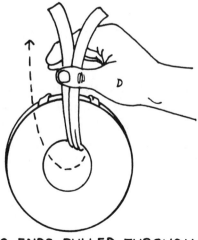

TWO ENDS PULLED THROUGH
HOLE IN SECOND RECORD—
THEN UP TO TOP

give them a slight downward tug, to "demonstrate" that the ribbon is tightly looped around the record.

Take up the second record with your right hand. Place the top side of the second record flat against the top side of the first, pressing them together to trap the loop of ribbon between them. Remove your left thumb from between the records and take a new grip with that thumb to hold both records together. With your right hand, draw the ribbon ends through the center hole of the second record, pulling them through from front to back.

Lift the two ends of ribbon together straight up to the top and remove your left hand. The two records now hang on the ribbons that are held at the top by your right hand. (The weight of the second record, resting against the hidden loop, holds them on the ribbon together.)

Display the records hanging that way as you talk about the "mobile." Then, take one end of the ribbon in your left hand, the other end in your right hand, and *gently* draw your hands apart. The hanging records will remain on the ribbon as long as they are kept *vertical*. But as soon as you spread your hands far enough apart so the records are *horizontal*, the hidden loop will pull free and the records will fall from the ribbon.

You can release the records whenever you wish, timing it to your patter. Spread your hands with a sudden little outward and upward snap of the ribbon and the records will pop up into the air and fall free to the floor while the ribbon remains stretched out between your hands.

LIGHTNING RING ON ROPE

How it looks

You show a large brass ring and hang it over the open palm of your hand. Then you take two ends of a rope in the same hand and hold the ends in full view, with the rest of the rope hanging down in a long loop.

"I'm about to do two things at once," you say, "both of which may seem quite impossible. Without letting go of the ends of the rope, I am going to tie a knot in the center of it. At the same time, I intend to pass this metal ring right through the rope and link it into the middle of that knot. And it all happens much faster than I can hope to explain it to you."

You take hold of the ring with your other hand, swiftly pull it down over the rope, and the ring instantly becomes linked and tied with a knot that appears at the center, as you say, "Just ... like ... that!"

What you need

A brass-plated ring about 5 inches in diameter (big enough to fit easily over your hand).
A 4-foot length of soft clothesline.

The secret

The rope and ring are unprepared. The trick is accomplished with one simple move that instantly forms a standard Ring Hitch.

LIGHTNING RING ON ROPE

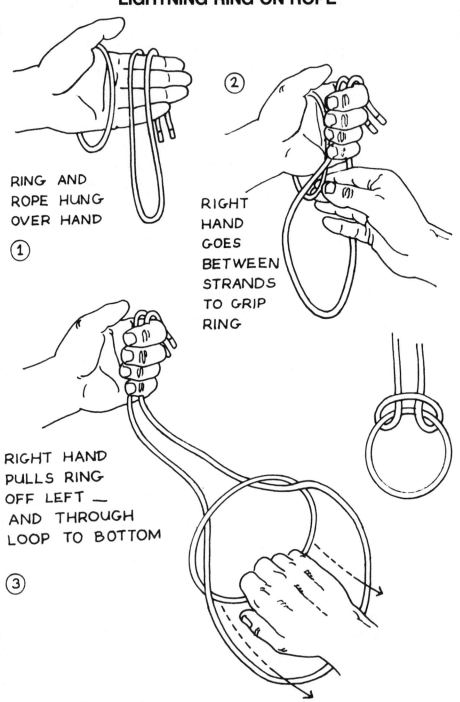

RING AND
ROPE HUNG
OVER HAND

①

RIGHT
HAND
GOES
BETWEEN
STRANDS
TO GRIP
RING

②

RIGHT HAND
PULLS RING
OFF LEFT —
AND THROUGH
LOOP TO BOTTOM

③

PENETRATIONS

What you do

Show the ring and turn your left palm up flat in front of you, thumb to the front, fingertips to the right. Hang the ring over the hand, close to the thumb. Take one end of the rope in each hand, hold it stretched out between them to show it, and bring both ends evenly together. Lay the two ends on your left fingers, to the far right of the ring, with the ends hanging over the front edge of the hand by a few inches so they will remain in full view, and the long center loop hanging down toward the floor.

Display the ring and rope lying separately on your outstretched hand. Then, close your fingers over the parallel strands to hold them tightly, and lift your hand with its back to the audience and palm toward you. What you do now should all be performed in one swift, continuing motion. Bring your right hand over beneath your left hand. Slide your right fingers *in between the two strands* and grip the *bottom* of the ring with them. Pull the ring to the right, off your left hand, and then lift the bottom of the ring *up toward you through the strands*, and swiftly pull the ring down to the bottom of the loop. (This automatically forms the Hitch that knots the rope around the ring.)

Give the ring a quick downward tug to tighten the knot that now holds it tied at the bottom of the loop and take your right hand away. *Immediately* bring your right hand up to take one of the top ends of the rope from your left hand. Spread your hands apart to show the ring knotted at the center of the rope stretched between them.

After the trick is over, be careful about how you

untie the ring from the center of the rope in front of the audience. Don't do it by simply pulling out both strands of the Hitch together, because that gives the trick away by revealing that what looks like a "knot" is only a simple Hitch. Untie it by drawing out one strand at a time, as if you were untying an ordinary Overhand Knot.

COMEDY SOAP AND ROPE

How it looks

"We come now to the educational part of this program," you say. "Here's a household hint that can save you a little money—and make it safer to take a shower."

You hold up a large bar of soap that has a rope threaded through a hole cut in its center. The rope is tied in a loop, and you untie it and remove the soap.

"You all know what shower soap is—the kind you hang around your neck so that when the water is splashing in your face you don't have to grope for the soap," you say. "Most shower soap is expensive; but you can easily make your own at home. Just take any cake of soap, cut a hole through the center with a kitchen paring knife, and string it up on a rope. Tie the rope through twice, like this."

As you explain, you demonstrate by threading the rope through the soap, and again tying it into a loop, which you put over your head so the soap hangs down in front of you. "There you are. You've got your own inexpensive shower soap in your favorite brand." You hold up the roped bar. "But there *is* one problem with shower soap. When you've got it hanging around your neck like this, how do you reach down with the soap to wash your toes?"

You awkwardly show how hard it would be to reach down to your feet with the soap. "Of course, you could untie it from the rope," you say. "But there's a simpler way. You just use magic ... and pull the soap right through the rope!" Suddenly you pull the bar of soap free from the loop that hangs around your neck. "There it goes ... And now you can wash your toes!"

What you need

A 5-foot length of soft clothesline.
A large (bath size) bar of soap.
A sharp-pointed kitchen paring knife.
A penny.
White cloth adhesive tape.
A ruler.

The secret

The ends of the rope are switched during their threading through the soap, secretly doubling the rope upon itself and forming a small loop. The loop is drawn inside the hole where it jams into a position that keeps the soap on the rope until you are ready to release it.

With the ruler, find the center of the soap, front and back. Press the penny into the soap, first one side and then the other, to mark a circle around those centers, and cut the hole through with the knife.

Bind each end of the rope with a short horizontal strip of white tape, to prevent fraying and to make it easier to thread the rope.

COMEDY SOAP AND ROPE

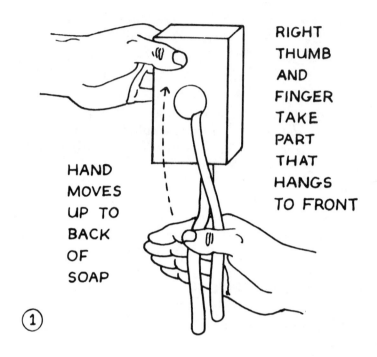

RIGHT
THUMB
AND
FINGER
TAKE
PART
THAT
HANGS
TO FRONT

HAND
MOVES
UP TO
BACK
OF
SOAP

①

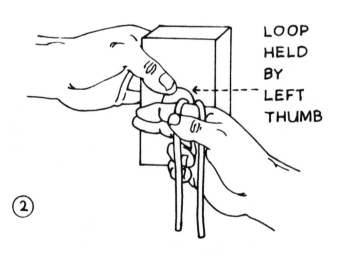

LOOP
HELD
BY
LEFT
THUMB

②

RIGHT HAND
MOVES BACK TO
TAKE OTHER END

③

AFTER
BACK END
HAS BEEN - - - →
PUT
THROUGH
LEFT
SIDE
OF HOLE

④

Put one end of the rope through the hole from back to front. Draw half the length of the rope through, bring it around the bottom of the soap, and then put that *same end* through the hole from back to front again. Bring both ends to the top and tie them into a loose Square Knot, so the soap hangs at the bottom of the long loop.

The soap is now really tied on the rope and that is the way you first show it to the audience, so they can watch you untie it, which helps convince them that the later retying of it is genuine.

What you do

Start by showing the soap tied on the rope. Untie the top knot, unloop the rope, and remove the soap from it. After explaining about the "shower soap," what you seem to do is tie it back on the rope in the way it was tied before. The following moves should be practiced until you can do them smoothly and deliberately, without hesitation.

Hold the soap upright with your left hand, fingers at the front around the left edge, and thumb at the back just above the center hole. Take one end of the rope with your right hand and push it through the hole from back to front. Draw the rope out until the two ends hang even at the bottom. Move your right hand, with its palm toward you, down about 2 inches below the bottom of the soap. Bring that hand around *both parts* of the hanging rope, so they hang down through your fingers.

Grip the part of the rope that hangs down from the *front* of the soap between your right thumb and first finger and move your right hand straight up against the back of the soap to just above the center hole. This forms a little loop across the top of your right first finger. Put that loop under the tip of your left thumb and hold it with that thumb against the back of the soap.

Leave that part of the rope hanging and slide your right hand back toward you along the *other part* of the rope to the end of it. Take that other end and push it from back to front through the left side of the hole in the soap. Draw that end out through the hole to the front until it draws the little loop into the hole. Continue to pull that end *gently* forward until the little loop is jammed inside the hole.

Bring both ends of the rope to the top, tie them into a Square Knot, and put the loop over your head so the soap hangs on the rope in front of you. Joke about the problem of trying to wash your toes while the soap is tied around your neck.

"Of course, you could untie it from the rope," you say. "But there's a simpler way." Take the bar in your right hand. "You just use magic . . . and pull the soap right through the rope!" As you speak, pull the bar out toward the right, away from the rope, and it will come free, leaving the tied loop still hanging around your neck. "There it goes . . . And now you can wash your toes!"

WITH A LOOP OF STRING

This is magic using only your hands and a simple loop of string. It's a series of penetrations all based on the ancient puzzle-like trick of seeming to pull a string through the thumb, but with variations that build it into an amusing little close-up routine.

How it looks

You hang one end of the loop over your thumb, wind the string around it, and ask someone to hold up one of his thumbs. Dropping the other end of the loop over his thumb, you have him pull on the string as he counts aloud. At the count of "three," he magically pulls the string right through your thumb, so your thumb is free and the loop is left hanging from his.

Taking the loop from him, you wind it around the back of your hand and give him the other end to hold. Once more, he works the magic, and tugs the string through your hand. You then hang it over your wrist, wrap it around, and he pulls it through your arm.

What you need

A 30-inch length of Venetian blind cord, or other smooth-finished and pliable string.

The secret

Basically, each of the penetration tricks depends on the same move, but done somewhat differently each time—a secret figure-eight twist that reverses the strands and lets you control the release of the string. The only preparation is to tie the ends of the string together with a small and tight Square Knot, and to trim the ends off close to the knot.

What you do

Through the Thumb

With the palm of your left hand toward you and the thumb upright, hang the unknotted end of the loop over the thumb. Bring your right hand under the bottom end of the loop, palm upward and fingertips toward the left. Put those fingers up through the loop from left to right, closing your hand around it. Lift your right hand up until the loop is stretched horizontally between your hands.

Twist your left fingers in toward you, hook the tip of your second finger over the strand nearest to your body, and pull that strand back over the top of the other one and around to the back of your thumb. Immediately turn your partly closed left hand palm downward. With your right hand, hang what is now the forward strand over your left thumb, and then draw the string taut between your hands again.

Reversing the strands has formed a small loop around the tip of your left second finger, hidden now by the closed fingers of that hand. Press that secret loop against the base of your left thumb and keep it held there until the end of the trick. At this point, the doubled string has really been just bent around your thumb, although the thumb appears to be firmly bound.

Ask someone to hold up one of his thumbs. Put the right-hand end of the loop over his thumb. Tell him he is about to perform the magic and explain that he is to pull on the string with his thumb while he counts aloud to three. At his count of three, secretly release the little loop from under your left fin-

THROUGH THE THUMB

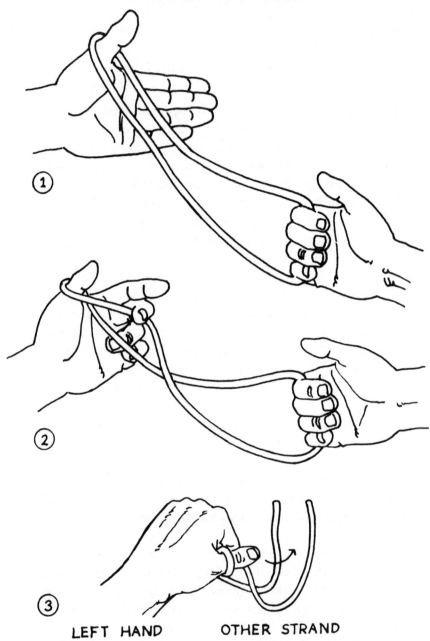

LEFT HAND
TURNS DOWN

OTHER STRAND
PUT OVER THUMB

ger so the string pulls free from your thumb and hangs from his. "You've pulled it right through my thumb," you say. "Now that you know how to do it, let's try something a little more difficult."

Through the Hand

Take the string from the spectator. Turn your left hand palm downward, thumb pointed toward you and fingertips toward the right. Hang the unknotted end of the loop over the back of that hand, so that the rest of the string hangs down beneath it. (The loop should *not* encircle the thumb, which is kept free.) Bring your right hand, palm down, to the bottom end of the loop. Put your right fingers down through it, from right to left, and close them around it.

Bend your left fingers down and catch the side of your left second finger against the outside of the strand that is nearest to your body. With that finger, pull that strand out away from you, over the top of the other strand, and then hook that same fingertip down between the two strands.

Without pausing, lift your right hand, with its end of the string, straight up above the back of your left hand. This automatically brings part of the string up inside your left hand. Close your left fingers into a loose fist. Inside the fist there are now two little loops caught around the tip of your second finger. Each of the strands has been doubled upon itself, and all that holds the string around your hand is your finger in those loops.

Have the spectator take hold of the top end of the loop, the part your right hand has been holding a

THROUGH THE HAND

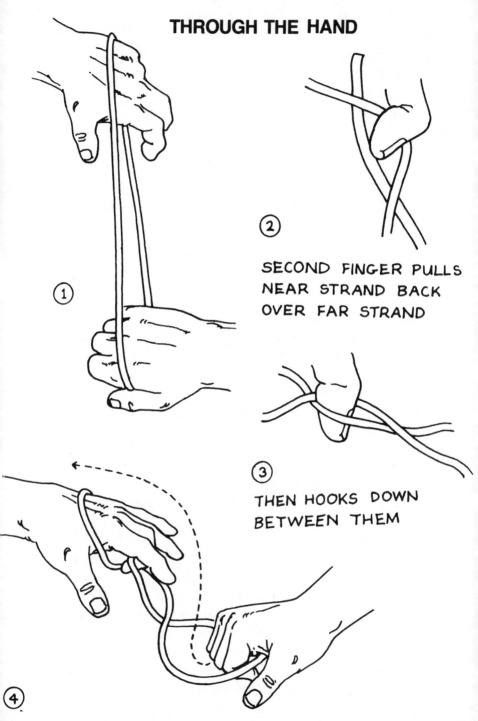

①

② SECOND FINGER PULLS
NEAR STRAND BACK
OVER FAR STRAND

③ THEN HOOKS DOWN
BETWEEN THEM

④
RIGHT HAND BRINGS ITS END UP OVER BACK OF LEFT

THROUGH THE WRIST

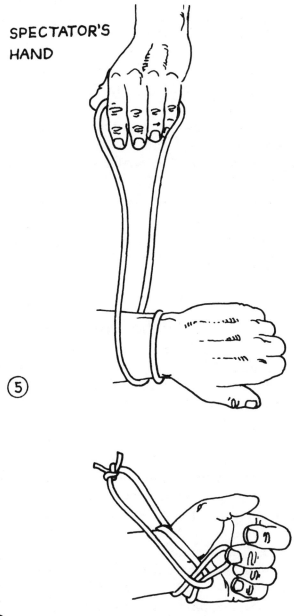

SPECTATOR'S HAND

⑤

⑥ VIEW FROM UNDERNEATH

few inches above the back of your left hand, and remove your right hand.

"I want you to imagine you are a magician who is about to perform the illusion of sawing a woman in half," you say. "How would you pass the solid blade right through her body without causing her any harm?"

As you speak, lift your left hand slightly, so the string between your hand and the spectator's is slack. Suddenly open your left hand out flat, fingers straight and wide apart. This pulls the little hidden loops off your fingertip so the string seems to pass through your hand and comes free, leaving it hanging from his hand. "That's the idea," you say. "You've done it! ... But I'm just as glad you didn't use a saw!"

Through the Wrist

"This time, I'll bind my arm and you can help me escape," you tell the spectator. Take the string from him and hang the unknotted end over your left wrist just above your hand. Turn your left hand palm down.

Take the bottom end of the loop with your right hand by putting your fingers down through it. Keep the loop taut and lift your right hand up to the right until it is horizontally opposite the left hand.

Catch the side of your left second finger against the outside of the strand that is nearest to your body and then hook that same fingertip down over the far side of the other strand. Draw that finger up against the base of the left palm and close your left hand into a fist. Lift your right hand, with the end of the loop it is holding, up over the back of your left hand and out to the wrist. (This doubles the strands upon themselves and forms a small hidden loop at the tip of your left second finger, which it holds tightly pressed to the base of the left palm. The string can be tugged, but won't pull free until you are ready to release it from your finger.)

Give the spectator the knotted end from your right hand, and say, "All you have to do now to work your magic and free me is just to pull the string *gently* .... Pull it right through my arm." Let him tug at the string once or twice, and tell him, "Maybe you should say some magic word. Why don't you say the name 'Houdini'?" Have him pull on the string again as he says "Houdini," and release the string so it suddenly "penetrates" your arm and comes free.

4

~~~~~~

CUT AND RESTORED

IMPROMPTU REPEAT CUT ROUTINE

This direct, fast-moving routine has been planned to keep both the rope and your hands in action during the two minutes or so it takes to perform—it gets right to the point of cutting and restoring a rope twice without any distractions from the simple main plot. The first cutting sets things up for the second cutting, and it can be done almost anywhere, with no advance preparation.

How it looks

With one end of the rope held in your left hand, you run your open right palm out along the rope to the center, bring the center to your left hand, draw it up into a loop, then lift the other end up beside it. You cut through the center, take two ends in each hand, and spread your hands apart to show the two cut pieces. Touching the four ends together so the hanging pieces form a circle, you immediately shake out the rope to show it whole again.

You then take one of the ends in your left fist and lift the center of the rope up to the level of your head. Holding the center between the right thumb and first finger, you pull the end out of your left fist so it swings out and down to hang beside the other end. Bringing the center over to your left hand, you again cut the rope in two and continue to snip pieces off it, cutting it several times. Looping the rope once, you draw it out between both open hands to show it restored once more.

What you need

While any reasonable length of soft clothesline or even thick cord or string can be used, the cutting will leave the rope several inches shorter at the end of the routine than it was at the start, so it is best to begin with a piece about 6 feet long.

Sharp round-ended scissors that will fit into your jacket pocket.

The secret

Both parts of the routine depend on variations of long-standard sleight of hand methods of cutting and restoring a rope. The moves have been simplified so they shouldn't be difficult to learn, but it will take practice to learn to do them smoothly. The first part of the trick leaves you with an extra-short piece, which becomes the loop that you cut through and snip away for the second restoration, so that at the end you again have a plain length of rope.

What you do

Each part will be explained as a separate trick, first the *End to End* effect and then the *Cut and Trim*. Either part can be used as a trick by itself, if you prefer not to show a repeat cutting. Start with the scissors in your right-hand jacket pocket and have the rope in the pocket with them, or else keep it handy on your table.

End to End

Take one end of the rope in your left hand, with the back of the hand toward the audience. Hold the end clipped between the side of the thumb and base of the first finger so that about 2 inches of the end extends above your hand.

Turn your right hand palm up, out flat, fingertips to the front and thumb opened out to the right. Bring that palm up under the rope and close to your

END TO END

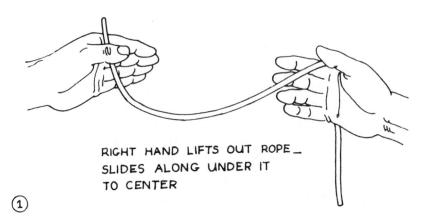

RIGHT HAND LIFTS OUT ROPE —
SLIDES ALONG UNDER IT
TO CENTER

①

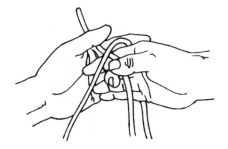

RIGHT SECOND FINGER HOOKS
PART OF LEFT END

②

REAL
CENTER

FINGER
PULLS
END
PART
UP AS
LOOP

③

CUT
HERE

BOTTOM END_
BROUGHT TO TOP

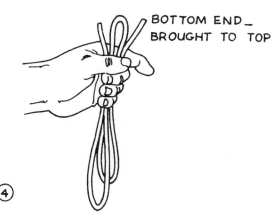

④

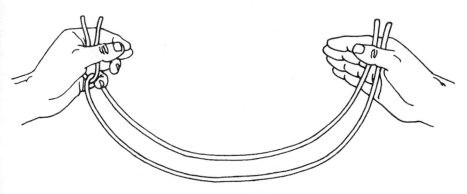

TWO ENDS IN EACH HAND

⑤

continued on next page . . .

END TO END—continued

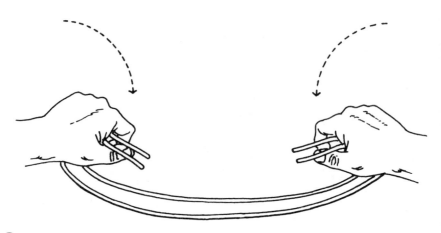

⑥   HANDS TURN IN TOWARD EACH OTHER

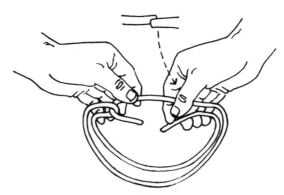

HANDS COME TOGETHER — RIGHT THUMB PRESSES
OVERLAPPING LEFT AND RIGHT ENDS AGAINST
⑦   INSIDE OF FINGERS

left hand, so the rope hangs down over the right edge of the fingers. Lift the rope out to the right by sliding the open palm along the underside of it to the center. Then, turn that palm toward you, fingertips to the left, leaving the free end of the rope hanging down over the back of the right fingers.

Bring your right hand over inside the left palm and, as your hands come together, hook the right second finger under the part of the rope that hangs down beneath the left thumb. Tilt the right fingers down behind your left hand so the center of the rope slides off them, and then immediately lift your right hand up, drawing the part that is hooked over the second finger into a small loop that extends about 2 inches above your left hand. Close the left fingers to hold the loop and remove your right hand. (In a simple and natural way, you have secretly switched the center of the rope for the small loop formed by one end. The real center now hangs at the bottom of that loop, hidden behind your left palm. Your left hand appears to be holding one upright end of the rope, with the center loop extending up beside it.)

Without pausing, bring your right hand down and take the bottom end of the rope. Lift that end up to place it to the right of the loop and hold it with the other end and loop in your left hand. Then, take the scissors from your pocket with your right hand. Cut through the center of the upright loop and spread the cut ends apart. Drop the scissors, points down, into your outer breast pocket.

You seem to be holding four rope ends with your left hand. With your right hand, take the two ends that are at the right, gripping them between thumb and fingers. Continue to hold the other two ends with your left hand and spread your hands apart so the rope hangs slackly between them. With two ends in each hand, show the two "cut-in-half" pieces.

The restoration should happen quickly, as though you merely touch the four ends together in a circle for an instant, then shake out the rope to show it whole again. Here is how it is done:

Holding two rope ends in each hand, turn both hands in toward each other, palms down, and left thumb opposite right thumb. Bring your hands together so the sides of the left and right first fingers touch. This also touches the four ends together.

Grip what is now the *forward* left rope end and the *forward* right end together between your right thumb and first finger. Slide the thumb to the right to squeeze those overlapping ends against the inside of your right fingers and hold them tightly as one. Drop the other ends and the rest of the rope completely from both hands and lift the right hand up and out to the right to hold it high. Shake out the rope to show it restored. (Your closed right hand conceals the overlapping pieces so that the extra cut piece, hanging out of the hand, looks like the top end of the rope.)

Cut and Trim

The restored rope now hangs down from your right hand, with the overlapping pieces pressed against the inside of the fingers by the tip of the thumb. The visible end of the cut piece should hang out of the top of your right hand *toward the audience*. (If it doesn't, shake your hand a little to flop the end over in that direction.)

Lift your left hand up in front of you, palm to-

IMPROMPTU REPEAT CUT ROUTINE
CUT AND TRIM

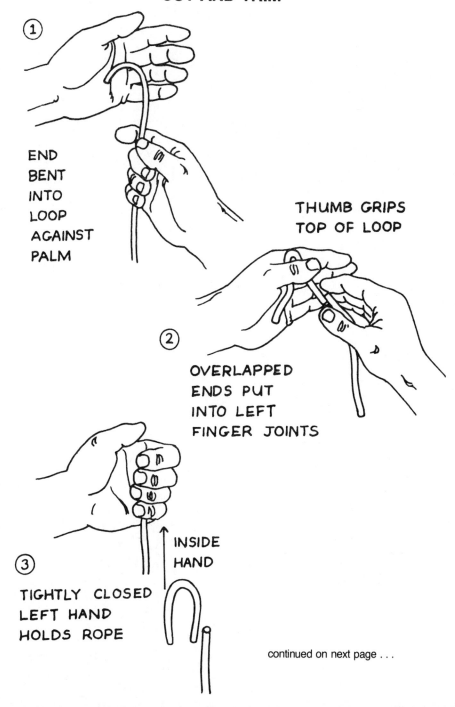

① END BENT INTO LOOP AGAINST PALM

THUMB GRIPS TOP OF LOOP

② OVERLAPPED ENDS PUT INTO LEFT FINGER JOINTS

INSIDE HAND

③ TIGHTLY CLOSED LEFT HAND HOLDS ROPE

continued on next page . . .

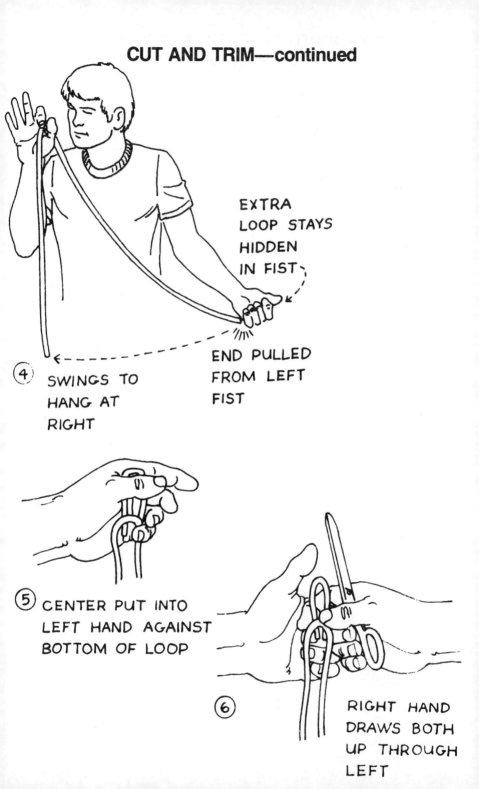

EXTRA
LOOP STAYS
HIDDEN
IN FIST

END PULLED
FROM LEFT
FIST

④ SWINGS TO
HANG AT
RIGHT

⑤ CENTER PUT INTO
LEFT HAND AGAINST
BOTTOM OF LOOP

⑥

RIGHT HAND
DRAWS BOTH
UP THROUGH
LEFT

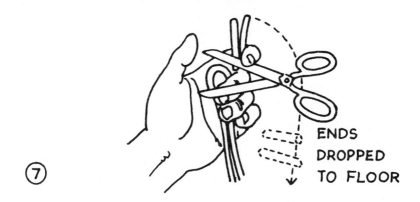

ENDS
DROPPED
TO FLOOR

⑦

BLADES HELD FLAT TO PRETEND
CUTTING LAST PIECES

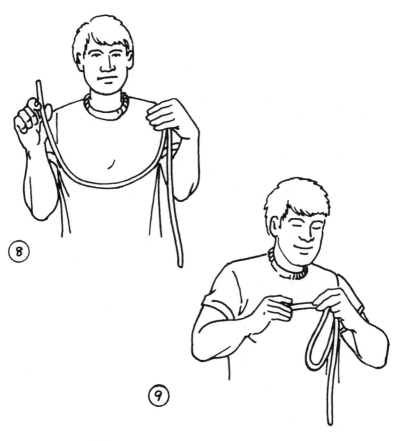

⑧

⑨

FRONT VIEWS

ward you, and fingertips to the right. Bring your right hand down to the left. Touch the end of the cut piece against the base of the left palm so the end folds over to form a small loop across the inside of the palm, and close your left thumb over the top end of that loop. Without pausing, place the overlapping parts against the middle joints of your two lower left fingers. Quickly close your left hand into a fist to hold the rope as you remove your right hand. (The bending of the cut piece into a small loop happens almost automatically as you push the hanging end against the left palm. The transfer of the overlapping parts from your right thumb and fingers to the joints of your left fingers leaves the real top end of the rope tightly gripped against the inside bottom of the left fist.)

Now, grip between the right thumb and first finger the rope that hangs beneath your left fist. Run these fingers out along the rope, lifting the rope out to the right. Turn your head to the right and look at that thumb and finger, to fix attention on them as they continue to slide out to the center of the rope. Keep your left fist, holding its end of the rope, in front of your chest, and lift your right hand up to the level of your head, with the center of the rope gripped between thumb and finger.

As you draw the upward-slanting rope taut between your hands, pull on the center with the right thumb and finger, giving it a little tug, and release the end from the bottom of the left fist so it swings out free and drops beside the other end that dangles down from your right hand.

Turn your head to glance at your breast pocket, as if looking for the scissors. Bring your right hand down to your left hand, opening your left fingers enough so you can put the center of the rope into that hand against the bottom of the hidden loop. Close your left fist again to hold them both, and immediately reach with your right hand and take the scissors from your breast pocket.

Hold the scissors, handle end down, loosely in your right palm, leaving your thumb and first finger free. With the right thumb and first finger, reach down inside your left hand, opening the left fingers to let you grip both the lower part of the extra loop and the top part of the real center. Draw them up until most of the extra loop extends above the top of the fisted left hand and the real center is just below the inside of the left first finger. Press the left thumb against the finger to hold them there.

Hold your left hand chest-high so the loop can be seen clearly. With your right hand, bring the blades of the scissors over behind the loop. Cut the loop in two through the center. Then, cut a piece off each of the cut ends. Move the scissors down, so the blades are partly below the left first finger, keeping the blades flat against the cut loop. *Pretend* to cut twice more, as though still trimming bits off the rope, but really just work the scissors. Lift the left thumb and let the remaining pieces of the extra loop drop to the floor as the other cut pieces did.

Drop the scissors back into your breast pocket. You are still holding the real center of the rope doubled inside the left fist. With your right hand, pick up one of the rope's bottom ends. Bring it up to hold it between your left thumb and first finger. Remove your right hand for a moment and turn your fisted left hand palm down, thumb toward the right. Take the same end between the first finger and thumb and *slowly* draw the rope out to the right, pulling it through your left hand as that hand slides along the rope to the left. Grip the rope between the left first finger and thumb, opening the other fingers wide, and hold it out between both hands to show it is whole again.

RING A STRING

How it looks

"Here's a little puzzle you might want to put together to show some of your friends," you say, as you take out a small ring and a long string. "I should warn you that it's a puzzle with a catch to it." You thread the string through the ring, then bring the bottom end up to the middle and tie a knot. Holding the string by its top end, so the ring hangs at the bottom of the knotted loop, you explain, "Now this is the puzzle. ... How can you get the ring off the string without untying the knot or breaking the string?"

You let watchers think about it for a moment, and then say, "The answer is—that you cheat a little." Reaching into your pocket, you take out a small pair of scissors and cut through the string, letting the ring slide free to the table. You hold up the cut string with its two pieces knotted at the center. "I said 'without *breaking* the string.' I didn't say anything about not *cutting* it."

As if you had finished explaining the puzzle, you quickly wind the string around your fingers. "It's a silly little stunt. But it is fun to do at a party. If you show it to your friends, just keep them guessing for a minute before you bring out the scissors." You drop the scissors back into your pocket. "Of course, it does leave you with a string that has been cut in half. But that's another problem—and the way to solve that ... is with magic!"

You snap your fingers over the cut string and unwind it, to show that the knot has vanished and the string is whole again. "The ring has been removed and the string is all in one piece," you say. "So I didn't *really* cheat—well, not *much!*"

What you need

A 3-foot length of soft, smooth-finished cotton string.

A small ring.

Small scissors with round-ended blades that will fit easily into a jacket pocket.

The secret

The loop is tied in a way that makes it look as if you are cutting through the center of the string, but you really cut one end. Then, you secretly slide the knotted cut piece off the string as you wind the string around your other hand, and you get rid of the knot when you drop the scissors back into your pocket.

There is nothing to prepare in advance. Just have the scissors in your right-hand jacket pocket and the ring and string in another pocket. (This is a close-up trick that should be performed near a table or counter that you can rest the ring upon.)

What you do

Explain that you want to show those who are

RING A STRING

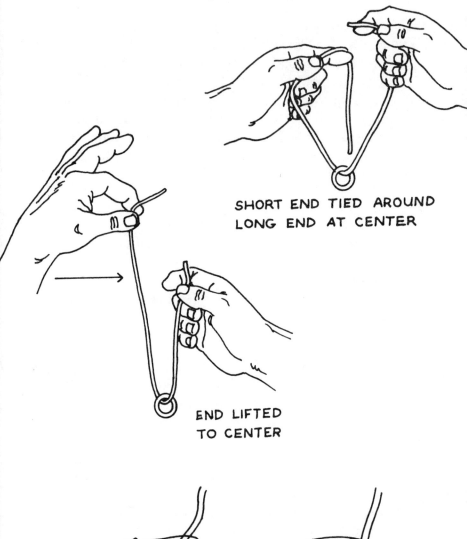

SHORT END TIED AROUND
LONG END AT CENTER

END LIFTED
TO CENTER

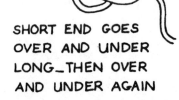

SHORT END GOES
OVER AND UNDER
LONG_THEN OVER
AND UNDER AGAIN

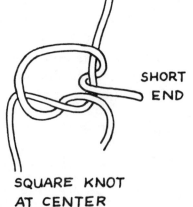

SHORT
END

SQUARE KNOT
AT CENTER

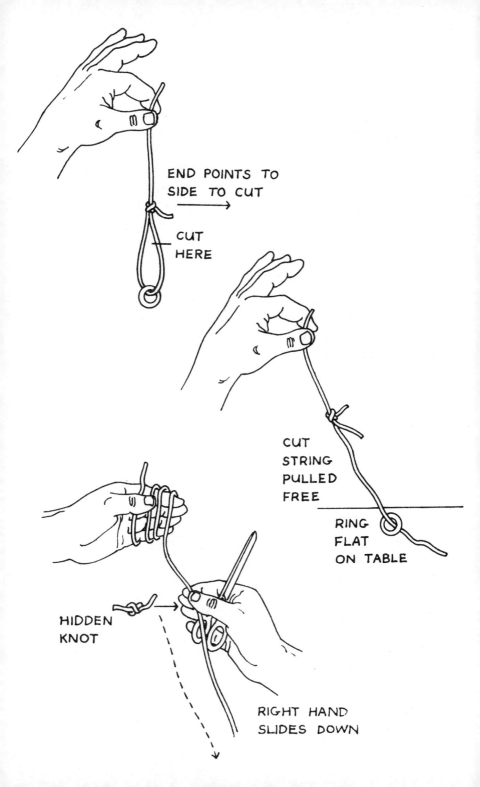

END POINTS TO
SIDE TO CUT

CUT
HERE

CUT
STRING
PULLED
FREE

RING
FLAT
ON TABLE

HIDDEN
KNOT

RIGHT HAND
SLIDES DOWN

watching a little puzzle that they may enjoy showing to others, and take out the ring and string. Thread the ring on the string, take one end of the string in each hand, and slide the ring back and forth a few times, finally letting it slide down to the bottom end held by your right hand. Lift your left hand straight up so the string is vertical and bring the right end up next to the center of the string.

Hold both strands with your right hand for a moment and drop the top end from your left hand. Bring your left hand down to take the left strand of string again at the center. Use both hands to tie the short right-hand end into a *Square Knot* around the center. (It must be a genuine Square Knot because the trick won't work with any other knot. Just tie the short end *over and under* the long end, then *over and under* the long end again.)

After the knot has been tied, slide your left hand up to hold the top end as before and remove your right hand to leave the string hanging down from your left hand. The ring hangs at the bottom of the loop formed by the knot tied at the center. Explain that the puzzle is how to get the ring off the string without untying the knot or *breaking* the string. Wait a moment, as if you were really offering a puzzle to be solved, and then say, "The answer is—that you cheat a little."

With your right hand, reach into your pocket, take out the scissors, and click the blades as you show them. Lower your left hand so the ring at the bottom of the string rests flatly on the table. (This is so it won't fall to the floor after you cut the string.) Cut through the *one side* of the loop that has the *end of the knot* sticking out from it, making the cut about an inch below that knot. (It makes no difference how the string may have twisted after the knot was tied, as long as you remember to cut through the strand *below* where the end of the knot sticks out. That end "points" to the side that should be cut. If you cut the other side of the loop, the string will really be in two pieces!)

Keep the scissors loosely held in your right hand. With your left hand, draw the string up so the ring comes free and remains lying on the table. The hanging string appears to have been cut in half, with the two parts knotted at the center. Explain that the catch to the puzzle was not to *break* the string, "but I didn't say anything about not *cutting* it."

Act as if the stunt were over, so that restoring the string will come as a surprise. With your left hand still holding the top end of the string, bring your right hand around the knot at the center. Close your fingers around it, pressing the knot against the inside of the fingers with the thumb. Lift the string and quickly wind it up around the extended fingers of your left hand, sliding your right hand down along the string as you wind it, and secretly sliding the knot down with it. As you finish the winding, the knot will slide right off the end of the string into your closed right hand.

The fact that you still have the scissors in your right hand provides a reason for keeping the hand closed and helps hide the knot. It looks to those watching as if the knot had been wound into your left hand with the rest of the string. Just as you secretly slide the knot off the end, lift your right hand and gesture with the scissors, as you say, "If you show it to your friends, keep them guessing for a minute before you bring out the scissors."

Drop the scissors into your pocket and leave the knot there with them as you turn your head and look at the string wound around your left hand, lifting that hand a little to fix attention on it. "Of course, it does leave you with a string that has been cut in half," you say. "But that's another problem—and the way to solve that . . . is with magic!"

Snap your fingers over the string and unwind it. Take it between your hands to show that it has been restored. Point to the ring lying on the table, and say, "The ring has been removed and the string is all in one piece. So I didn't *really* cheat—well, not *much*!"

TOSS AND CUT

How it looks

You take a small ball of rope from your pocket, toss it from hand to hand, showing both hands empty, then shake out the rope to uncoil it. Holding the rope dangling straight down from one hand, you bring the other hand to the center and draw the rope up through that hand. Picking up a pair of scissors, you cut through the center of the rope and cut away several pieces, but as you stretch the rope out it instantly becomes whole again.

What you need

A 3½-foot length of soft clothesline with the core removed.
A 6-inch piece of the same clothesline.
Scissors.

CUT AND RESTORED

The secret

As with many other such tricks, you cut through a loop made of the extra piece instead of through the real center of the rope. But the whole thing is self-contained and there is nothing to hide in your hands at the start or to get rid of at the end. The ball of rope is fixed to deliver the extra loop into your hand when and where you need it, by the simple action of taking away the rope with the other hand to uncoil it.

Bend the small piece of rope into a loop with the two ends touching at the bottom. Lay one end of the long rope vertically on top of the small loop so that end extends 2 inches above the loop.

Take the part of the long rope that is just below the loop and start winding it around the loop and the end. Wind it around in four flat turns, then continue winding the rest of the rope upon those first turns until you have a small ball. All the windings should be kept toward the bottom of the loop so that the loop and the top end of the rope stick up out of the center of the ball. Use the point of the scissors to tuck the last end of the rope in under one of the strands to hold the ball together.

Put the ball of rope into the right-hand pocket of your jacket and have the scissors on your table.

What you do

Take the ball of rope out of your pocket with your right hand and show that your left hand is empty. Toss the ball from your right hand into the left and show the right hand empty.

TOSS AND CUT

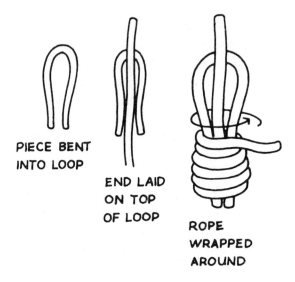

PIECE BENT
INTO LOOP

END LAID
ON TOP
OF LOOP

ROPE
WRAPPED
AROUND

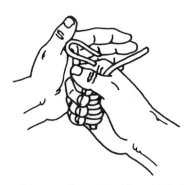

RIGHT HAND DRAWS ROPE DOWN
OFF LOOP CLIPPED UNDER LEFT THUMB

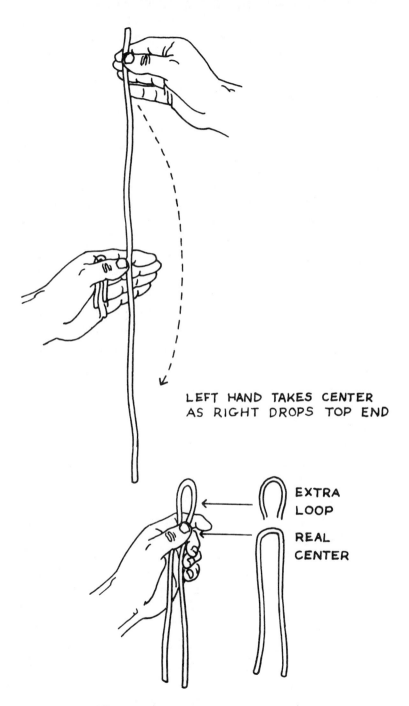

LEFT HAND TAKES CENTER
AS RIGHT DROPS TOP END

EXTRA
LOOP

REAL
CENTER

DRAWN UP THROUGH HAND
AND HELD FOR CUTTING

Hold the back of your left hand toward the audience and bring your right hand to the palm of the left to take the ball of rope. As your hands come together, push the top end of the loop that is sticking out of the ball into the crotch of your left thumb. Press the side of your thumb over the loop to hold it tightly. Then, close your right fingers around the ball and draw it down away from your left hand. This draws the ball down off the extra loop, which remains clipped under your left thumb.

Lift your right hand high and give it a sharp downward shake to uncoil the ball so the rope hangs straight down from that hand. Bring your left palm against the center of the hanging rope. Hold the center between the tip of your left thumb and first finger. Release the top end of the rope from your right hand and let it fall back and to the bottom. Close your left fingers into a loose fist, which brings the real center of the rope over against the extra loop hidden inside the hand.

With your right thumb and fingers, reach into the top of your left hand and draw the extra loop up so the top of it extends well above the hand. Hold it there with your left thumb.

Pick up the scissors with your right hand. Cut through the fake center loop and spread the two ends apart so everybody can see it has been cut. Then, continue to snip little pieces off each of the cut ends until the entire extra loop has been cut away.

Keep your left hand as it is, with the real center of the rope inside it. With your right hand, take one of the bottom ends of the rope and hold it straight up above your left fist. Rub the center of the rope with your left fingers, give it a little tug, and open your left hand wide to show that the rope has been restored to one piece.

DOUBLE DOUBLE

How it looks

You show a rope, draw it freely through your hands, and then hold it so it hangs straight down from one hand. Your other hand moves about one-third of the way down the rope, brings that part up into a loop, then moves down again and brings up a second loop.

With scissors, you cut through one loop and then the second loop, seeming to cut the rope into three parts. Folding the cut ends down into your hand, you snap the fingers of your other hand and instantly stretch the rope out between them to show that it is fully restored.

What you need

A 4½-foot length of soft white clothesline.
A second piece of clothesline, 10 inches long.
White cloth adhesive tape, ½ inch wide.
Scissors.

The secret

The short piece of rope is made into a double-looped gimmick with the adhesive tape; part of it also forms a small tube that slides up and down on the long rope. This permits a casual handling of the rope, as well as the instant restoration after the two fake loops have been cut.

Lay the long rope vertically on a table. Cut off a 10-inch length of tape and turn it *sticky side up*. With the sticky side out, wrap the tape upon itself, twice around the rope at a point about 4 inches up

DOUBLE DOUBLE

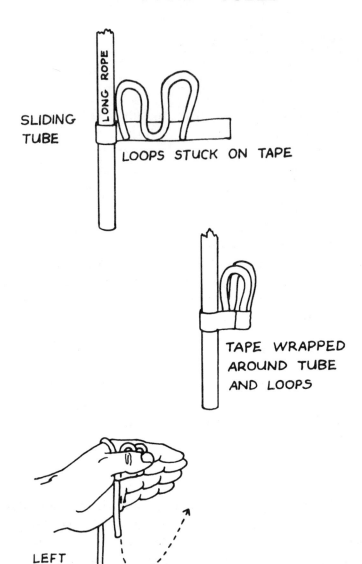

SLIDING
TUBE

LONG ROPE

LOOPS STUCK ON TAPE

TAPE WRAPPED
AROUND TUBE
AND LOOPS

LEFT
HOLDS
SLIDING
GIMMICK

RIGHT HAND PULLS
DOWN AND HOLDS
OUT TO FAR RIGHT

①

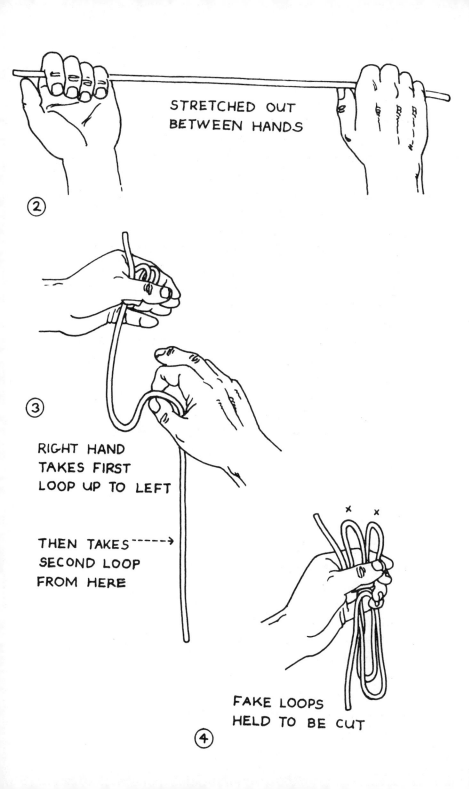

STRETCHED OUT
BETWEEN HANDS

②

③

RIGHT HAND
TAKES FIRST
LOOP UP TO LEFT

THEN TAKES- - - - →
SECOND LOOP
FROM HERE

FAKE LOOPS
HELD TO BE CUT

④

from the bottom end. The tape should be wrapped so that the small tube it forms slides easily on the rope. Bring the remainder of the tape, sticky side up, out to the right of the rope on the table.

Take one end of the short piece of rope and stick it firmly to the tape just to the right of the little tube. Form a loop about 2½ inches high and bring the right side of that loop down to stick it to the tape. Then, form a second similiar loop beside it and bring the other end down to stick that to the tape. Fold the tape toward you so that the second small loop is on top of the first one. Wrap the rest of the tape tightly around the tube and the bottom ends of the attached loops.

Keep the gimmick positioned on the rope about 4 inches up from the bottom end and with its two fake loops upward. Take the gimmick in the palm of the left hand. Fold the rest of the rope loosely back and forth upon it and put it into the left-hand pocket of your jacket. Have the scissors handy on the table where you can pick them up with your right hand.

What you do

Take out the folded rope with your left hand so the gimmick is against the palm and hold that hand in front of you with its back toward the audience. Unfold the rope with your right hand and drop the long part of it down over the back of your left hand.

Bring your right hand down to the short end of rope at the bottom of your left hand. Take that short end with your right hand and draw it horizontally out to the far right until all but a few inches of the rope has been pulled through the bottom of your loosely fisted left hand, drawing it through the sliding gimmick that remains hidden in your left hand. Hold the rope stretched out between both hands to show it.

Drop the rope end from your right hand and let that end swing down toward the floor. Hold the rope high with your left hand. Bring your right hand to the hanging rope about one-third of the length down from the top and take it between the right thumb and first finger. Lift that part up as a loop and place it inside your left hand against the bottom of the hidden gimmick, holding that loop with your lower left fingers. Again, bring your right hand down along the rope, move it lower down, and lift it as a second loop to hold with the first one inside your left hand.

With your right thumb and fingers, reach down into the top of your left fist. Draw the two fake loops up into view until the band of tape at the bottom of the gimmick is against the inside of the left first finger. Separate the two loops a little so they can be seen clearly and hold the gimmick in place there with the left thumb.

Pick up the scissors with your right hand. Cut through the center of one of the fake loops and separate the two cut ends. Then, cut through the center of the second loop and separate those ends. Put down the scissors and display the twice-cut rope with your left hand. Bring your right hand, palm toward you, to the *front* of your left hand and bend the four cut ends back down together into the left fist, closing the left fingers around them.

Lift your right hand away from the rope, hold it high and snap your fingers twice, as if "casting a spell" to restore the rope. With your right hand, take the hanging bottom end of the rope and pull it down and out to the right to unfold it quickly and show it whole, stretched horizontally between your hands.

Drop the rope end from your right hand and let it swing toward the floor. Then, take the top end with your right hand and draw the rope out through your left hand far enough to hold it stretched between both hands again. Finally, gather the rope with your right hand, put it into your left hand, and put the loosely folded rope away in your jacket's left pocket.

5

LONG AND SHORT

LIGHTNING STRETCH

How it looks

"Give a magician enough rope and he'll do a rope trick," you say. "But I'm embarrassed to tell you that when I packed my things for the show, I forgot to give myself enough rope." From your pocket, you take out a rope less than a foot long. "This little scrap is too short to be much use for anything."

You bring the two rope ends together to show how short it is, then measure it around the open palm of your other hand. "It hardly goes around my hand." Holding the short rope so it hangs down from that hand, you take one end and pull it out through the hand. Instantly it stretches to more than three times its original length, as you say, "What I really need is a piece about *this* long!"

What you need

A 3½-foot length of soft clothesline with the core removed.

A nail file.

The secret

Most of the rope is folded upon itself into a small bundle that hangs between the two ends, and it is handled so it looks from the front like a little scrap of rope, until you pull it out to full length.

Start 6 inches from one end and fold the rope up and down in tight 1½-inch accordion folds until you are about 10 inches from the other end. Then, take the 10-inch end and wind it *tightly* twice around the accordion folds, crossing the second turn down over the first to hold the folds together. Finally, make a small loop and push it up under the wound-around strands, using the round end of the nail file.

You should now have two short ends, with the folded bundle hanging securely between them. Put the rope into the right-hand pocket of your jacket.

What you do

Reach into your pocket, get the bundled part of the rope into the palm of your right hand, close the fingers around it, and bring that hand out in front of you with its back toward the audience. Use your left hand to adjust the rope by drawing the top end up until the bundle is just beneath the crotch of your right thumb. Close the thumb to hold it there, drop the end over the back of your right hand, and remove your left hand.

With the bundle hanging hidden behind your right palm and the two ends in view, it looks from the front like a little piece of rope. Take the bottom end of the rope with your left hand and bring it up to hold it for a moment with the tip of your right thumb, showing both ends together at the top and a short loop hanging beneath your right hand, and say, "This little scrap is too short to be much use for anything."

Release that end and let it fall to the bottom again, so you are holding the rope as at the start. Give your right hand a little *inward* shake, toward your body, to toss the top end back so it falls over the top of the right thumb and hangs to the inside of the right hand.

Bring your left hand, palm toward you, over inside your right hand. Grasp the top end of the rope, just above the bundle, in the crotch of your *left* thumb, and turn both hands out to the left *together* as you turn your body slightly in that direction. As you turn your hands, bring the left palm toward the audience, release the bundle from your right hand so it is hidden *behind* the left, and immediately move your right hand down from in back of the left to take the bottom end of the rope with your right hand. Without pausing, lift that bottom rope end to bend the rope up over your left palm, and say, "It hardly goes around my hand." Drop that rope end and remove your right hand as you extend your left palm

LIGHTNING STRETCH

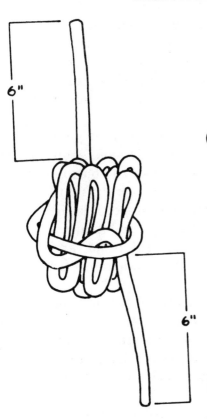

6"

6"

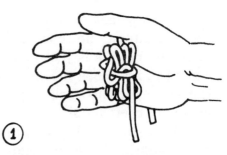

①

HELD BY THUMB

BACK

②

BOTH ENDS BROUGHT UP

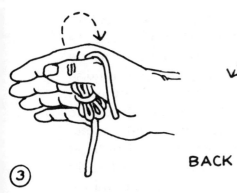

③

HAND SHAKES END
OVER TOP OF THUMB

BACK

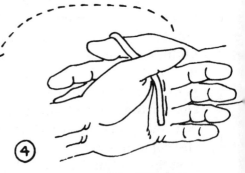

④

LEFT THUMB TAKES —
BOTH HANDS SWING OUT
TO LEFT TOGETHER

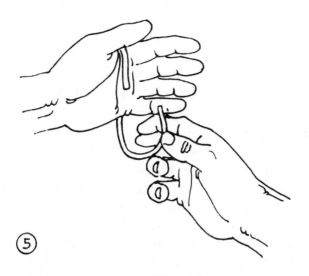

⑤

BUNDLE NOW HIDDEN
BEHIND LEFT HAND _
"IT HARDLY GOES AROUND MY HAND."

FRONT

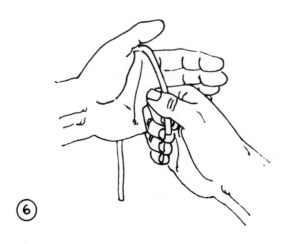

⑥

RIGHT HAND PULLS END

higher and farther out to the left. At this point, the top end is held under your left thumb, and the rope hangs down the back of the hand, with its folded bundle still hidden from front view behind the left palm. Keep it held that way for a moment to display the "little piece" of rope.

Then, bring your right hand up and take the top end of the rope, keeping your left hand as it is, palm toward the front. With your right hand, pull the end straight out and down from your left hand, closing the left fingers around it as it passes through. As you quickly pull out the top end, the bundle pulls loose against the back of your left thumb. The rope magically "stretches" to full length between your spreading hands, and you say, "What I really need is a piece about *this* long!"

RIBBON STRETCH

How it looks

You show a 2-foot length of bright-colored ribbon and tie its ends together to form a small loop. Taking one side of the little loop in each hand, you see-saw your hands up and down and gradually "stretch" the loop until the ribbon is 9 feet long.

What you need

A 3-yard length of bright-colored ½-inch satin ribbon.
A nail file.

The secret

Part of the ribbon is folded upon itself into a small bundle which is hidden by your hands. The way you hold the ribbon and secretly add to its length from the bundle gives the illusion of stretching it.

Start about 8 inches from the ribbon's top end and flatly fold it up and down upon itself in 1-inch accordion folds. When you have folded all but about 16 inches, wind it *tightly* around the folded bundle twice, in flat turns, and tuck about a 1-inch loop under those turns, using the round end of the nail file.

Have the prepared ribbon on your table behind some other prop that hides it from front view, so that you can quickly get it into proper position in your right hand before you hold it up to show the audience.

What you do

The ribbon should be held in your right hand so that the part of it just above the secret bundle lies at the crotch of your thumb, gripped there by the thumb. The top end of the ribbon hangs down over the back of the hand, which is toward the audience, and the bundle hangs hidden inside the palm, with the bottom end of the ribbon hanging straight down.

Hold it up that way to show what looks like a 2-foot length of ribbon. Let it be seen that your left hand is empty and bring that hand over to the inside of your right hand to take the ribbon. Do this by closing your left fingers into a loose fist around the bundle, so it is hidden within the three lower fingers,

RIBBON STRETCH

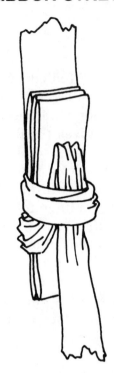

① TIGHTY WOUND AROUND
AND TUCKED UP UNDER

SECRET
BUNDLE

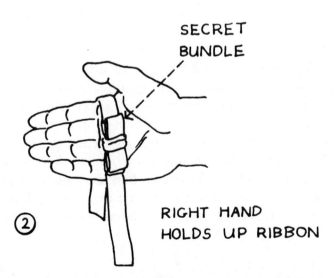

② RIGHT HAND
HOLDS UP RIBBON

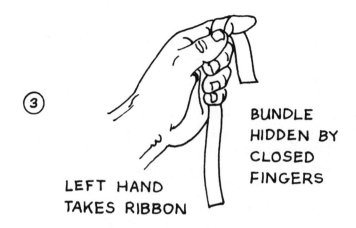

③ **LEFT HAND TAKES RIBBON**

BUNDLE HIDDEN BY CLOSED FINGERS

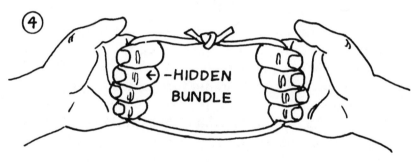

④ **—HIDDEN BUNDLE**

HANDS HOLD UP SMALL LOOP

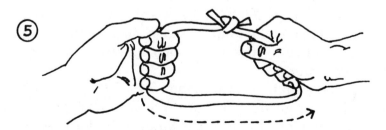

⑤ **TURNING RIGHT HAND PULLS SOME OF HIDDEN RIBBON FROM LEFT HAND**

with the ribbon's top end hanging out over your first finger.

Immediately bring your right hand down to the bottom end of the ribbon. Lift that end up and lay it across the end that extends from the top of your left hand. Hold the crossed ends beneath your left thumb. With the help of your right hand, tie the two ends together in a tight Square Knot.

Take the right side of the little loop with the right hand by closing that hand into a loose fist around it. Hold up the loop to show it between your two fisted hands. You now pretend to stretch the loop as you tilt your fisted hands back and forth and very slowly draw them apart.

Tilt your right fist over toward the left until its thumb points to the left, pulling on the *bottom* part of the loop as your fist turns, which pulls a little of the ribbon from the bundle hidden inside your left fist. Then tilt your left fist over toward the right. Continue to tilt one fist and then the other, pulling a little on the bottom of the loop each time you tilt the right fist, rocking your fists back and forth. As you do that, keep sliding your right fist down its side of the loop so that the knot remains centered at the top, between your hands.

All of this is done in one continuous series of motions, rocking your hands back and forth until the full loop is stretched out. Finally, open both hands wide and display the giant loop hanging between your two thumbs.

If you wish to use the ribbon for a follow-up trick in a ribbon routine, you can untie the ends quickly. Just pull one end to upset the Square Knot and slide it free.

GREAT GRANDMA'S MAGIC THIMBLE

How it looks

"There's a story in our family that my great grandmother owned a magic thimble," you say, as you reach into your pocket, bring out a thimble and show it, and put it back into your pocket again. "She was also the family's champion string saver. She never threw away any little scrap of rope or string."

You hold up three short pieces of clothesline that are knotted together at both their top and bottom ends. After unfastening them at the top to show three separate pieces, you knot two of them together again, tying them end to end. Then, you repeat the same process with the bottom ends, tying two of those together, so that the three tied pieces are strung out end to end.

"Whenever great grandma had saved a few little pieces, she would tie them all together, end to end, and wind the pieces into a ball," you explain, as you wind the knotted rope around one hand. "Then she would take out her magic thimble . . ."—reaching into your pocket, you bring out the thimble on the tip of your first finger—". . . and tap the tied-together little pieces three times—just like this."

You tap the thimble three times on the rope wound around your other hand. "And instead of just a few scraps, there would be one long rope—all put together as good as new." Quickly you unwind the rope to show that the knots have vanished and the three pieces have magically joined together as one. " 'Waste not, want not,' she always used to say."

What you need

A 6-foot length of soft clothesline.
Two additional pieces of clothesline, each 6 inches long.
A thimble.

The secret

The long rope is doubled, with one of the little extra pieces looped through each doubled end, so at the start you seem to have three tied-together short ropes. The extra pieces, after being tied as "knots," are secretly stolen away in your hand when you wind the rope around your other hand. The "magic thimble" provides a logical reason for reaching into your pocket to get rid of the extra pieces, so that at the end you are left with only the plain length of rope.

Prepare the rope in advance by laying it out vertically on a table and doubling it into three separate sections, with one loop at both top and bottom. Thread a short extra piece of rope through each of the end loops, bending the short pieces so their ends come together next to each real end of the rope.

Hold the top set of three "ends" together and tie all three with one wrap-around single knot. Draw it tight to conceal the looped part within the knot. Tie the bottom set of three "ends" together in the same way. You now have what looks like three short lengths of rope, tied together top and bottom so the audience will see three ends at the top and three more at the bottom. Have the prepared rope on your table and the thimble in your right-hand slacks pocket.

LONG AND SHORT

What you do

As you talk about "great grandmother's magic thimble," reach into your pocket, get the thimble on the tip of your right first finger, bring it out to show it, and then put it back into your pocket. This plants the idea right at the start that you later will be reaching into your pocket to bring out the thimble again. Explain that "great grandma" also saved scraps of rope and string, and hold up the "three" tied-together pieces to show the audience.

Use both hands to untie the large knot at the top, keeping your hands together so as not to reveal that two of the "ends" really are one looped short piece. Take the ropes in your left hand, between your thumb and fingers, with the back of the hand toward the audience. Your thumb covers the bottom of the short loop and the three "ends" extend above the top of your hand.

With your right thumb and first finger, lift the real end of the long rope out to the right. Hold it for a moment to show that the pieces are separate. Then drop that end, let it fall to the bottom, and remove your right hand. That leaves your left hand holding only the two ends of the short piece and the looped part of the rope that hangs beneath.

Bring your right hand back to your left hand and with both hands tie the short rope piece in a single knot around the rope. Keep the small loop hidden by your fingers until the knot is tied and then show the knot. This looks as if you had tied two of the ropes together, end to end.

Now, take the remaining large knot at the bottom and bring that to the top to untie it as you did

GREAT GRANDMA'S MAGIC THIMBLE

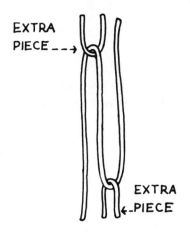

EXTRA PIECE ---→

←- EXTRA PIECE

①

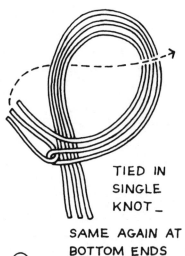

TIED IN SINGLE KNOT —

SAME AGAIN AT BOTTOM ENDS

②

③

THIMBLE IN POCKET

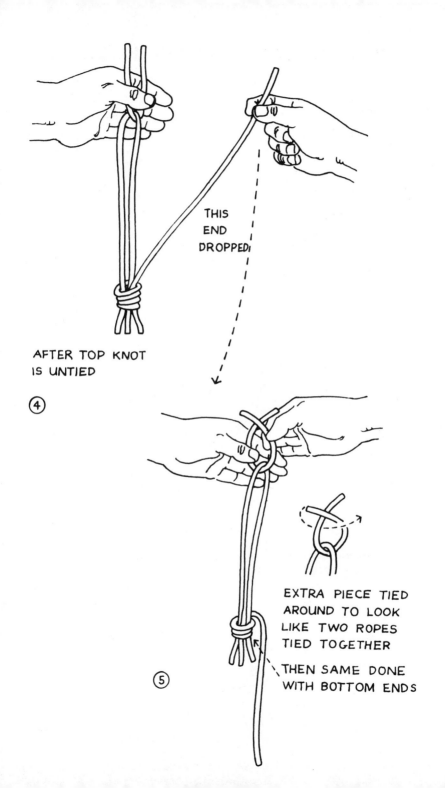

THIS
END
DROPPED

AFTER TOP KNOT
IS UNTIED

④

EXTRA PIECE TIED
AROUND TO LOOK
LIKE TWO ROPES
TIED TOGETHER

THEN SAME DONE
WITH BOTTOM ENDS

⑤

GREAT GRANDMA'S MAGIC THIMBLE—2

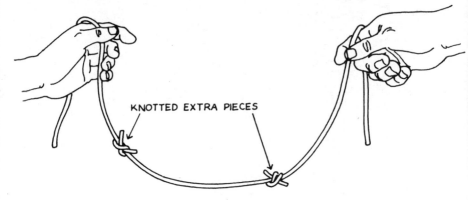

KNOTTED EXTRA PIECES

LOOKS LIKE THREE SHORT ROPES TIED END TO END

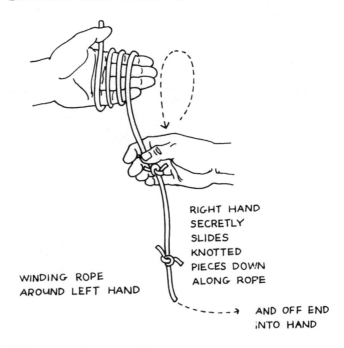

RIGHT HAND
SECRETLY
SLIDES
KNOTTED
PIECES DOWN
ALONG ROPE

WINDING ROPE
AROUND LEFT HAND

AND OFF END
INTO HAND

THE MAGIC TOUCH
OF GREAT GRANDMA'S
THIMBLE!

the first one. Repeat the same moves of holding the three "ends" between your left thumb and fingers, lifting the long end out to the right and dropping it to the bottom, then tying the short piece in a knot around the rope. Show what appears to be the three short ropes, knotted together and strung out end to end. (You really have one long rope, with the two little extra pieces tied along it to look like connecting knots.)

"Whenever great grandma had saved a few little pieces," you say, "she would tie them all together, end to end, and wind the pieces into a ball." Turn the palm of your left hand toward you. Hold one end of the rope with your left thumb and with your right hand begin coiling the rope around your left hand. As you wind the rope around your left hand, the hanging part naturally slides through the palm of your right hand, bringing first one of the knotted little pieces and then the second one into that hand.

Just keep both of the knotted pieces in the right hand, concealed by the fingers that are partly closed around the rope, and continue to slide the hidden knots down as your hand winds the rope. The audience thinks the knots are still on the rope coiled around your left hand.

As you finish coiling the rope, secretly slide both little pieces off the end of the rope into your right hand. Let that hand drop to your side for a moment with the two hidden pieces and lift your left hand high to show the coiled rope, as you say, "Then she would take out her magic thimble. . . ." Immediately put your right hand into your pocket to get the thimble the audience already knows is there. Leave the two rope pieces in your pocket, get the thimble on the tip of your right first finger, and bring it out to show it again.

The rest is simply acting out the story. Display the thimble as though it had some "magic power." Tap your thimbled finger three times on the rope coiled around your other hand. Then, unwind the rope and hold it out between your hands to show that the knots have vanished and the three short pieces have joined together as one.

ODD-EVEN ROPES ROUTINE

Magicians have invented scores of "patter" themes, moves and alternate plots for the popular trick of magically stretching a short, a medium-length, and a long piece of rope so that all three become the same length.

The presentation given here has been performed for more than twenty years before audiences of all ages, on stage, television, and in close-up magic. It sticks closely to the basic plot and deliberately keeps to the simplest, most direct method of accomplishing it. The trick itself will be explained first, followed by a working script of the patter and presentation.

How it looks

You show three pieces of rope, one a foot long, the second 2 feet long, the third 3 feet long. Holding the three pieces together with your left hand, you draw their top ends down over the back of that hand so those ends are even, then bring the three bottom ends up and hold all six ends with your left hand. You obviously still have three ropes of differing lengths: short, medium, and long.

Taking three ends in each hand, you spread your hands apart and visibly "stretch" the ropes until all three are the same length. You count them separately from hand to hand. But suddenly the ropes "shrink" again, so that you end the trick as you began it, with a short piece, a medium-length piece, and a long piece.

What you need

Three pieces of soft clothesline—1 foot, 2 feet, and 3 feet long.

The secret

The short rope is secretly looped around the long one behind your left hand and the ends are placed in that hand so that when the ropes are "stretched," the long one becomes doubled in half, with the short piece looking like two top ends.

Lay the three ropes side by side, short, medium and long, with the top ends even, and tie those ends together with a single wrap-around knot. They can be carried that way until you are ready to perform the trick.

What you do

Untie the ropes, hold each one up to show it, and turn the palm of your left hand toward you, fingertips to the right. Place the top end of the short rope under your left thumb, close to the crotch, then place

ODD–EVEN ROPES ROUTINE

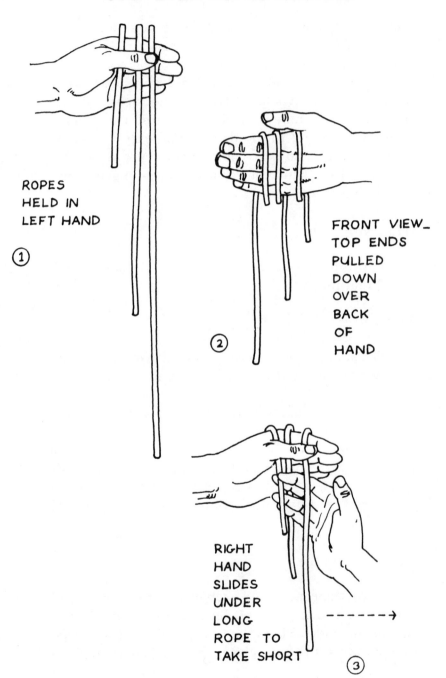

ROPES
HELD IN
LEFT HAND

①

FRONT VIEW—
TOP ENDS
PULLED
DOWN
OVER
BACK
OF
HAND

②

RIGHT
HAND
SLIDES
UNDER
LONG
ROPE TO
TAKE SHORT

③

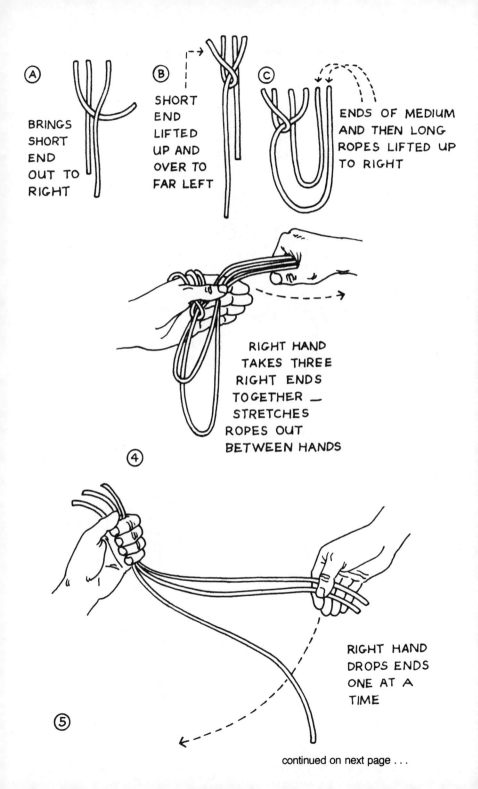

Ⓐ BRINGS SHORT END OUT TO RIGHT

Ⓑ SHORT END LIFTED UP AND OVER TO FAR LEFT

Ⓒ ENDS OF MEDIUM AND THEN LONG ROPES LIFTED UP TO RIGHT

RIGHT HAND TAKES THREE RIGHT ENDS TOGETHER — STRETCHES ROPES OUT BETWEEN HANDS

④

RIGHT HAND DROPS ENDS ONE AT A TIME

⑤

continued on next page . . .

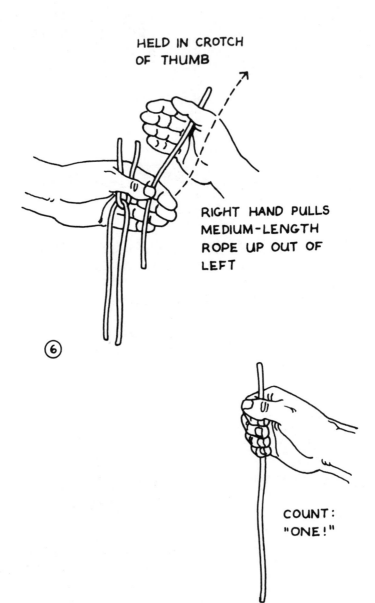

HELD IN CROTCH
OF THUMB

RIGHT HAND PULLS
MEDIUM-LENGTH
ROPE UP OUT OF
LEFT

6

COUNT:
"ONE!"

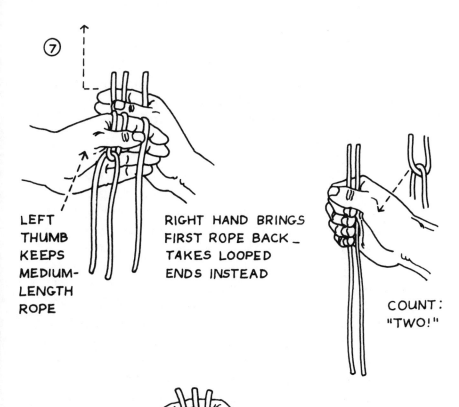

⑦

LEFT
THUMB
KEEPS
MEDIUM-
LENGTH
ROPE

RIGHT HAND BRINGS
FIRST ROPE BACK —
TAKES LOOPED
ENDS INSTEAD

COUNT:
"TWO!"

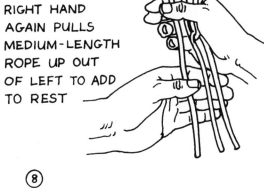

RIGHT HAND
AGAIN PULLS
MEDIUM-LENGTH
ROPE UP OUT
OF LEFT TO ADD
TO REST

⑧

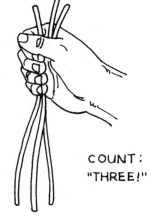

COUNT:
"THREE!"

the top end of the medium-length rope a little to the right of that, and finally, place the top end of the long rope to the right of both. The thumb holds all three pieces side by side, with about 2 inches of the ends extending above your hand.

Turn the left palm out to show the hanging ropes to the audience and then bring the palm toward you again. With your right hand, draw the three top ends down together over the back of your left hand until those ends are about even with the bottom edge of that hand. Pause to show that the three top ends have been drawn down to equal length.

Bring your right hand, fingertips to the left, over inside the left palm. Slide your right fingers *under* the long rope, *over* the medium-length rope, and grip the short rope just beneath where it is held by the left thumb. Lift the short rope out to the right, sliding the right fingers along to the end of it. Immediately bring that end up to the top and *over to the far left* to hold it with your left thumb, to the left of the other ends. Draw it down over the back of your left hand until that end is equal in length to the others. (You have secretly looped the short rope around the long one behind your left hand. This should look as though you simply took the hanging end of the short rope and brought it up to the top. Be careful to keep the hidden loop below your left thumb so the looping cannot be seen by the audience.)

Take the bottom end of the medium-length rope and bring that up to the *right* of the other ends, to hold that with the left thumb, and draw that end down over the back of your left hand until its length is equal to the others. Then, take the bottom end of the long rope and bring it up to hold it to the *right* of all the rest, drawing it down even with them.

Your left hand holds all six ends, which hang down at equal length over the back of that hand. With your right hand, separate the three ends that are to the right, so they are a little apart from the other three ends. Close your left hand into a loose fist around all the ropes and hold them up to show them as you remove your right hand.

You are now about to "stretch" magically the three ropes so they will visibly become the same length. Keep your left fist in front of you. Take the three top ends that are to the *right* with your right hand. Hold them together and draw your right hand horizontally out to the right, pulling the two hands apart as the loops seem to lengthen until all three ropes are equal. Keep the ropes as they are for a moment, so the audience clearly sees what has happened, and tug at the ropes stretched between your hands. Then, open your right hand enough so as to drop each of the rope ends separately and let them swing free to the bottom, one at a time.

Your left hand still holds what appears to be the other three ends, really the end of the medium-length rope and the two ends of the short rope that is looped through the center of the doubled long rope. Now, you seem to show each of the three ropes separately as you count them from hand to hand. But you "false count" them, in this way:

With the three top ends held by your left thumb, open the palm of your left hand toward you. Bring your right hand over against the *outside* of the left, so that the tips of the two lower right fingers touch against knuckles of the upper left. Grip the top end of the medium-length rope in the crotch of your right thumb and lift your right hand straight up to pull that rope completely out of your left hand, as you count aloud, "One."

Move your right hand back to your left hand as if to take a second rope, bringing both hands together again as they were, with the medium-length rope, which your right hand has just taken, hanging down inside your left hand. Press the tip of the left thumb against that rope to keep it in your left hand and grip the other two ends together with your right thumb and fingers. Draw those two ends straight up, closing your right fingers around the looped part to hide it, and pull those ropes out of your left hand, as you count aloud, "Two."

Now, take the remaining top end with your right hand and pull it up out of your left hand, as you count aloud, "Three." (This is really the medium-length rope that you are counting for a second time. You apparently have shown each rope separately as you transferred them from hand to hand.)

Keep the right fist closed around the ropes and hold them high to show that all three are of equal length. Wait for the applause, as if the trick were finished.

Then, put all three ropes together into your left hand, with the loop still concealed. Quickly take the three bottom ends with your right hand and bring those up to put them beside the other ends in your left hand. With your left palm toward you, open it enough so you can glance at the looping.

Take one of the short ends with your right hand and pull that short rope up out of your left hand, then take one end of the medium-length rope and pull that out, and finally pull out the long rope. Pass the ropes separately from hand to hand to show that they are once again as they were at the start: short, medium, and long.

Patter and presentation

Here is the full routine, in playscript form, for acting out the trick as explained:

Magician (speaks slowly, seriously): All of magic is make-believe, pretending, using your imagination. The whole of theater has its roots in that kind of magical illusion. When you go to a theater, you know that what happens on the stage isn't real. The scenery is painted, the words the actors speak are words that somebody wrote for them to say.

But if *you* pretend with them, if *you* make believe, then what happens on the stage seems real to you *while* it is happening. And that's the true joy of watching magic—making believe you can see something happen before your eyes that you know can't really happen at all.

(Picks up and unties the three ropes, shows each separately as he positions them in his left hand.) I'd like to show you what I mean with these three pieces of rope. There's a little piece, a middle-sized piece, and a long piece. *(Draws three top ends down over back of his left hand.)* If I were to draw these three ends down so they are equal, we might pretend, we might make believe, that we *have* three ropes that *are* the same length. *(Swings left palm out toward audience, runs right first finger down along each of the ropes.)* But we know we still have a little one, a middle-sized one, and a long one.

(Turns left palm toward himself again. Brings each of bottom rope ends up to hang evenly with top ends over back of his left hand.) If I were to bring *all* the ends up—the little one, the middle-sized one, and the long one—again, we might pretend that we have

three ropes the same length. (*Holds right palm flatly beneath the six hanging ends, as if measuring length, then gestures with right first finger toward the loops hanging beneath his left hand.*) But we know we still have a short loop, a medium one, and a long one.

(*Grips three right rope ends with his right hand. Stretches ropes between both hands, timing action to the words.*) Just for a moment, will you all *pretend* with me . . . that there *could* be such a thing as *magic* . . . that would *stretch* . . . these ropes to *be* the same length. (*Tugs ends between his hands. Lets right-hand ends drop down, one at a time. Brings right hand to left hand and counts ropes separately from hand to hand.*) One . . . two . . . three. (*Holds right hand high, fisted around ropes.*) Thank you for pretending with me that there *is* such a thing as magic.

Accepts applause as if trick were ended. Transfers ropes together from right to left hand. Brings bottom ends up beside top ends in left hand. Then pauses and smiles to audience.) But of course, we *were* just pretending, just making believe. (*With right hand, quickly pulls each rope separately out of left, holding them high to show them.*) Because there's still just a little piece . . . a middle-sized piece . . . and a long piece of rope.

6

***

ACROBATICS

THE ROPE THAT FLIES WILD

How it looks

You pick up a rope and a pair of scissors and hold the rope by its top end in your left hand and the scissors in your right hand, as if you were about to perform a rope-cutting trick. But the rope suddenly leaves your left hand and flies up through the air into your right hand. You put the rope back into your left hand, hold the scissors far out to the right, and once again the rope flies through space, across to your right hand.

"That one's too wild to use," you say, as you put the rope and scissors back on the table. "I'd better use a tamer piece." You then take another rope from your pocket and continue with your favorite cut-and-restored-rope routine.

What you need

A 3-foot length of soft clothesline.

Transparent colorless nylon thread. (Designed to blend with backgrounds of any color, this almost "invisible" thread is available at sewing counters in light and dark shades. The *light* shade is best for this trick.)

A small pair of scissors.

White cloth adhesive tape, ½ inch wide.

A needle.

The secret

The rope is pulled through the air from hand to hand by a pulley-like arrangement of the thread and scissors. While the thread is invisible from a short distance, this is not a trick to be shown to a close-up audience. It is self-contained, with no thread attached to your hands or body, and the threading is rigged so you can pick up the rope and scissors to present it at any time in your show.

Thread the needle with a 3-foot length of thread. Sew the thread to what will be the top end of the rope by stitching it through from side to side several times, and then remove the needle. Wrap a band of the white tape around the rope's end to prevent it from fraying and to hold the sewn thread more securely. Bind the bottom end of the rope with a similar band of tape.

Put the scissors points-upward on a table with the *finger-grip* part of the handle at the bottom left. Pass the free end of the thread down through that finger hole and then out to the left. Thread the needle with that end of the thread and push it through the rope from right to left about an inch below the rope's top end. Draw about 3 inches of thread out to the left and remove the needle.

Take a 2-inch length of the white tape and wind the end of the thread around it, sticking the thread to the tape. Then roll the tape upon itself and flatten it into a small button-like tab. (We'll call this the "end tab.")

To set it up for the performance, lay the rope at the left of your table, with its top end vertical and the end tab at the left. Draw the scissors out to the right as far as the thread will allow, and place them to the right of the rope, points toward the front.

What you do

Pick up the scissors with your right hand as you normally would if you were about to cut something, with your thumb through the thumb grip, second finger through the finger grip, first finger against the shank. Lift the scissors a few inches above the table and at the same time take the top end of the rope with your left hand, gripping it between the thumb and inside of the second finger so the little end tab lies horizontally under the thumb. (This is a natural way to pick up the rope and the positioning of the end tab under the thumb is automatic.)

Holding the rope with your left hand and the

THE ROPE THAT FLIES WILD

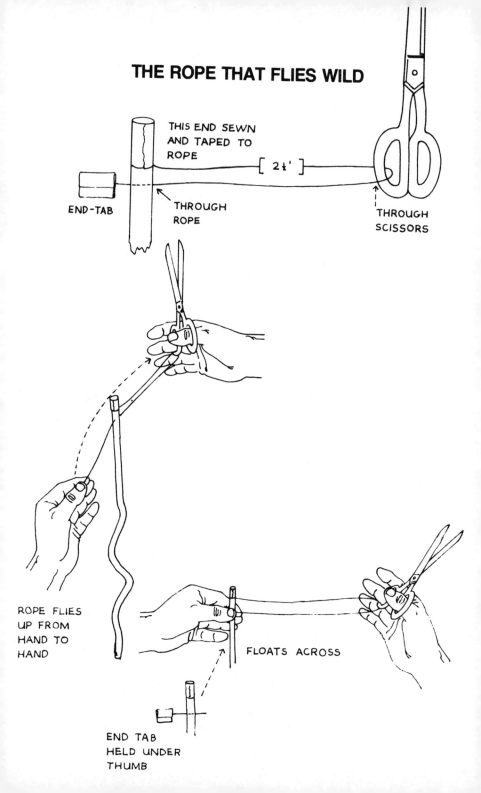

THIS END SEWN AND TAPED TO ROPE

[2½']

END-TAB

THROUGH ROPE

THROUGH SCISSORS

ROPE FLIES UP FROM HAND TO HAND

FLOATS ACROSS

END TAB HELD UNDER THUMB

scissors with your right hand, move away from the table. Keep the rope about waist-high with your left hand and move your right hand up and out toward the front, lifting the scissors high to display them. As your right hand sweeps up and forward, release the top end of the rope from your left hand, keeping the little end tab pressed against the fingers with the thumb. The rope will fly up from hand to hand, drawn by thread. (During this procedure, don't move your left hand at all; keep its fingers as they are. The rope will float up until its top end comes between the right thumb and second finger where they hold the scissors.)

Immediately bring your right hand back down to the left one. Grip the top end of the rope again between the left thumb and second finger, taking it from your right hand. Then, move your right hand with the scissors out to the right as far as the thread will allow. Release the rope from your left hand, keeping the end tab held under the thumb, draw your right hand out toward the right, and the rope will float across from hand to hand.

Bring your right hand back to your left hand and take both the rope and scissors with your left hand. Quickly gather the rest of the rope up into that hand and put the rope and scissors back on the table.

THE RING THAT FALLS UP

How it looks

You take a black ribbon and a brass ring from your pocket, thread the ring on the ribbon, and hold one end of the ribbon in each hand. Tilting your hands up and down, you slide the ring back and forth, so that it falls from the top to the bottom of the ribbon several times.

"When the ring falls *down*," you say, "that's gravity. But when the ring falls *up*...," and as you speak, the ring suddenly slides *up* the ribbon, from bottom to top, "... that's magic!"

What you need

A 20-inch length of black satin ribbon.

A brass-plated ring about 1½ inches in diameter.

Transparent colorless nylon thread. (The *dark* shade is best for this trick.)

A needle.

A small safety pin.

The secret

The method is an old one, used in many tricks of this kind. One end of the thread is fastened to the ribbon, the other end of the thread is attached to the performer. Moving the ribbon forward pulls the thread and causes the ring to rise. But the real secret of this version is in the way the thread is hitched up, so that it extends from below the level of your waist and directly out to the front from the center of your body. This keeps the thread well below the eye-level of the spectators, and centered against the solid background of your body, which helps to conceal it from those who are watching.

Since the reach of each person's arms is different, you will have to experiment to determine what length of thread best suits you, but start with a thread about 3½ feet long. Sew one end of it to one end of the ribbon, stitching it through several times so it holds firmly. Put the other end of the thread through the small hole at the bottom of the safety pin and knot it tightly.

Attach the safety pin inside the belt band at the center of the *back* of your slacks. Now, take the ribbon and pass it through your legs and out to the front, drawing the thread out between your legs. Put the ring into the otherwise empty right-hand pocket of your slacks. Then, roll the ribbon upon itself into a flat coil, starting with the *unthreaded* end, so as to leave the threaded end at the outside of the roll. Slide the rolled ribbon into your pocket on top of the ring.

With the gimmick set up this way, you can move around freely until you are ready to perform the trick. There is no attachment to the upper part of your body to interfere with the use of your hands or your jacket pockets while presenting other tricks.

What you do

Reach into your pocket with your right hand, take out the rolled ribbon, and bring it in front of you. Grip the end of the ribbon between the left thumb and first finger and give it a downward shake so the ribbon unrolls as you remove your right hand.

Keep the ribbon dangling down from your left hand. With your right hand, reach into your pocket again and bring out the ring to hold it high and show it. Thread the ring down over the top end of the ribbon and then hold both ring and ribbon together at the top end with the left thumb and fingers.

Bend forward slightly so you can reach down to

THE RING THAT FALLS UP

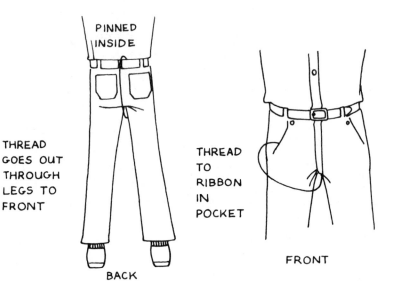

PINNED INSIDE

THREAD GOES OUT THROUGH LEGS TO FRONT

BACK

THREAD TO RIBBON IN POCKET

FRONT

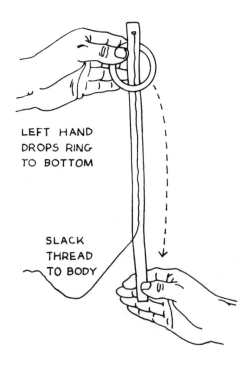

LEFT HAND DROPS RING TO BOTTOM

SLACK THREAD TO BODY

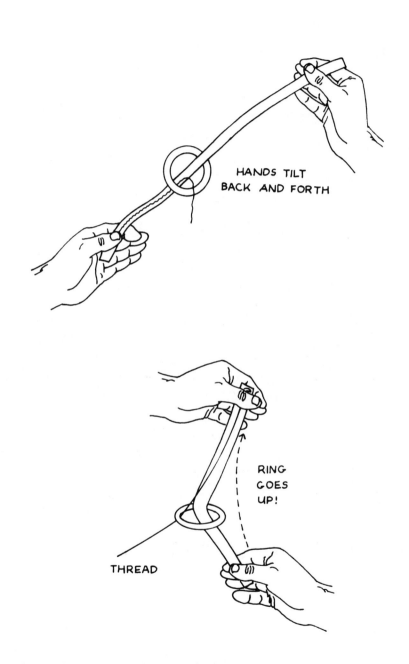

HANDS TILT
BACK AND FORTH

RING
GOES
UP!

THREAD

take the bottom end of the ribbon between the right thumb and first finger. Hold the ribbon taut vertically between your hands and move them both close enough to your body so the thread is slack. Drop the ring from your left hand and let it fall down the ribbon to your right hand at the bottom.

Still holding both ends of the vertical ribbon, bring your right hand up at the same time that you move the left hand down, so the ring again slides from top to bottom. Repeat this several times, tilting the ribbon and ring back and forth, as you say, "When the ring falls *down*, that's gravity."

Now lift your left hand so the ring and right hand are at the bottom of the ribbon, and say, "But when the ring falls *up* ..." Move both hands directly forward from your body, bending the top and bottom ends of the ribbon outward so the thread lifts the ring up the ribbon to the top. Grip the *ring* with your left fingers and drop the top end of the ribbon from your left hand to let it fall free, so the dangling ribbon now is held only by your right hand, as you say, "... that's magic!"

Gather up the ribbon with your right hand, put it back into the right-hand pocket of your slacks, and then take the ring from your left hand and put it away in the pocket with the ribbon.

SPOOKY ACROBATIC KNOTS

How it looks

You tie a large Bow Knot in a rope and hold the

rope by one end so the knot hangs at its center. Suddenly the rope seems to "come alive" and the knot magically unties itself.

Then, you tie a large Overhand Knot, hold the rope hanging down as before, and the bottom end of the rope rises up and spookily passes through the knot to untie the rope again.

What you need

A 2-foot length of soft clothesline.
Transparent colorless nylon thread.
A needle.
A thumbtack.

The secret

These two different knots that visibly untie themselves go well together. The first builds up the effect of the second, and both are worked by the simple means of a thread sewn to one end of the rope and tied at the other end to a thumbtack fastened under the top edge of the table. Secretly pulling up on the top end of the rope unties each of the knots.

Take a 2-foot length of the thread and sew one end of it securely to one end of the rope. Push the thumbtack into the underside of the table you will use when performing, close to its back edge, and knot the free end of the thread to the thumbtack. (The sewing and knotting shorten the thread, but about 1½ feet of it should remain between the end of the rope and the table edge.) Have the rope lying loosely on the table, with its threaded end toward the right.

What you do

Self-untying Bow Knot

Take up the rope near its center with both hands, palms *toward you*, and slide your hands out along it until they are about 8 inches apart. Grip the rope there between the thumb and first finger of each hand, so an end of the rope hangs down from each hand.

Holding it between the thumbs and first fingers, turn both hands palms *upward*, with the two little fingers side by side against the front center of the rope. Close the fingers of both hands down around the rope and turn the fisted hands inward toward each other until their knuckles touch together. This forms a large loop in each hand.

Slide the thumbs down to grip each loop at its base. Cross the left-hand loop over the right-hand loop and then tie the two together just as if tying an ordinary Overhand Knot. The result should be a Bow Knot with two big loops. (It is tied this way to avoid drawing any part of the thread into the knot or entangling it. The thread still runs directly down to the table from the right end of the rope.)

Hold up the rope by its two loops to show the knot, with the two ends hanging at the bottom. Take the left end of the rope between the thumb and first finger of the left hand and lift that hand so the rope hangs down from it, with the knot at its center. Bring the rope straight up above the table until the thread attached to the lower end is taut.

Point to the knot with your right hand and then snap your fingers. At the same time, secretly pull the top end upward with your left hand. This pulls out the two ends and the knot unties. (This should be done quickly, but without jerking the top end up. If the knot has been properly tied, only a slight upward pull is needed.) Hold the dangling rope for a moment and then let it drop from your left hand to the table.

Self-untying Overhand

Pick up the rope again with both hands, your left hand near the unthreaded end and your right hand near the end with the thread. Use both hands to tie a *large and very loose* Overhand Knot near the rope's center, bringing the threaded end out to the bottom. Holding the top end with your left hand, lift the rope above the table until the thread at the bottom is taut.

Point again to the knot with your right hand, and snap the right fingers. But this time, secretly pull your left hand up *slowly* so the audience can watch the bottom end of the rope gradually creep up and visibly pass through the knot to untie it. Hold the rope a moment longer and then let it fall from your left hand and drop back to the table. (Instead of attaching the end of the thread to the table, you may prefer to attach it to yourself. You can use the same sort of a hitch-up previously explained in this chapter for *The Ring That Falls Up* (page 183). Another method, with a slightly longer thread, is to attach the free end to your left shoe by tying it to a shoe strap, buckle, or shoelace eyelet. In either case, you would start with the rope, threaded end down, in your left pocket rather than on the table. At the end of the trick, you would put it away into that pocket again.)

SELF-UNTYING BOW KNOT

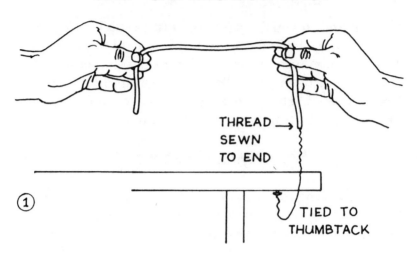

THREAD → SEWN TO END

① TIED TO THUMBTACK

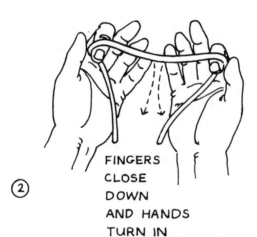

② FINGERS CLOSE DOWN AND HANDS TURN IN

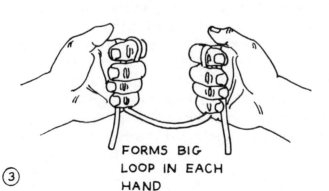

③ FORMS BIG LOOP IN EACH HAND

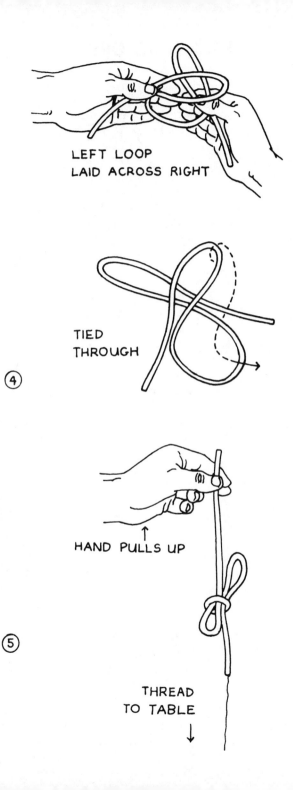

LEFT LOOP
LAID ACROSS RIGHT

TIED
THROUGH

④

HAND PULLS UP

⑤

THREAD
TO TABLE

SELF–UNTYING OVERHAND

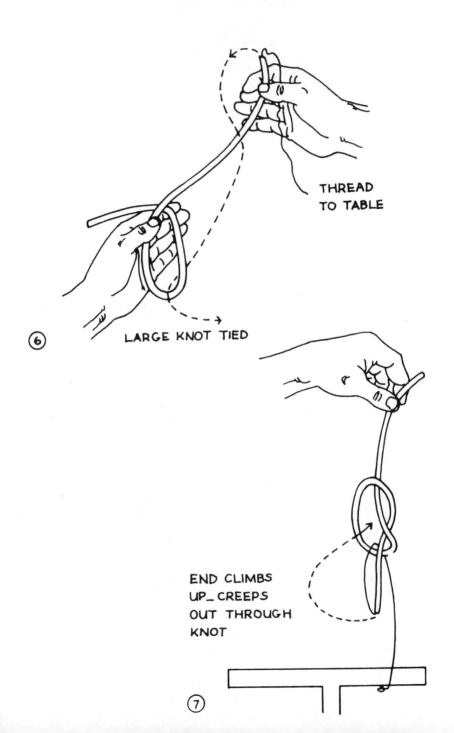

THREAD
TO TABLE

LARGE KNOT TIED

⑥

END CLIMBS
UP_ CREEPS
OUT THROUGH
KNOT

⑦

TOPSY-TURVY ROPE

In this comedy routine, the center of a rope visibly changes into the two ends of it and the ends join to become the center. This happens twice, and finally the one rope changes into two separate pieces, leaving no "center" at all.

How it looks

"For this trick, it is important to hold the rope at its exact center," you say, as you hold up a rope with one hand at its center, so the two ends hang down. "You can always find the center if you hold the middle at the top, because then the two ends have to be at the bottom." You bring your other hand up next to the hand holding the center. "I mean, if the two *ends* were at the *top*, then the *center* wouldn't be there because. . . ."

You break off your sentence as you draw your two hands apart. Suddenly, instead of holding the center of the rope, each hand holds one end, and the two ends that were hanging down visibly join together, so the separate ends are now at the top and the center is at the bottom. Pretending to be confused by what has happened, you say, "It's all upside down. Let me start again."

Running one hand down the rope, you again take it at the center, lifting that up as you drop the ends to the bottom, and say, "If I hold the center at the top, then naturally the two ends are at the bottom." But the same thing happens again. As you

draw your hands apart, you are holding two ends instead of the center, and the ends that were at the
bottom join to become the center.

"That's still upside down!" You shake your head
and look out at the audience. "Would you all please
stand on your heads for just a minute—so you can
watch this upside down? ... No, wait—I've got it
now."

You take the center of the rope with one hand
and drape the two hanging ends over the other
hand. "If I have two ends at the top and if I also have
two ends at the bottom—then I must have *four* ends
... and so I have!" You show that the rope has
changed into two separate pieces with four ends.
"But now, I don't know where the *center* went," you
say, as you throw the ropes down on the table. "And
that doesn't make any sense at all!"

What you need

Two 2-foot lengths of soft clothesline with their
cores removed.

Transparent colorless nylon thread.

Dull-finish (not shiny) transparent tape.

Scissors and a large needle with a big eye.

The secret

The thread runs through the center of the entire
lengths of both coreless ropes and is then tied into a
large circle, with a space between the ropes, so the
ropes slide on the endless loop of thread like two
tubes. When the rope's top ends are pulled apart, the
bottom ends lift and slide against each other, making it appear that they are joined as one piece.

Both ends of each piece of rope should be cut straight and trimmed clean so the ends will butt together evenly. Bind each end by wrapping transparent tape around it, winding it carefully so the outer edge of tape is even with the cut edge of the rope. Don't tape the ends so tightly that they are squeezed smaller than the rest of the rope; they should remain the same diameter.

Unwind a yard or so of thread from the spool, but leave it attached to the spool. Thread the needle and draw about a foot of thread through the eye so it won't pull loose. Take one of the ropes and push the needle into the hole at one end, where the core was removed.

Work the needle down through the center of the tube-like jacket by pushing it a few inches until the jacket bunches, then gripping the needle through the jacket and holding it while you smooth back the bunched rope. Continue in this manner until you can draw the needle and thread out from the rope's other end. Then, without removing it from the needle, work the same thread down through the center of the second piece of rope the same way, unwinding more from the spool as needed.

When the thread has been passed through both tubes of rope, slide the ropes together on the thread, draw about a foot of thread out at each end, and cut the thread from the spool. Hold both ends of thread together at a point where there will be about 9 inches of thread between the top ends of the two ropes. Tie the threads twice, making the knots with both strands held together, and trim off the excess thread about an inch above the knots. Then, slide one of the ropes around until the knots are inside that rope.

TOPSY-TURVY ROPE

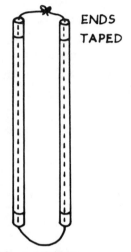

ENDS
TAPED

THREAD LOOPED
THROUGH BOTH ROPES

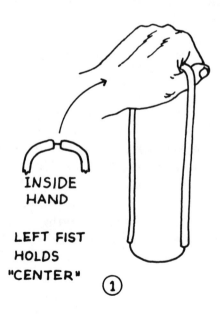

INSIDE
HAND

LEFT FIST
HOLDS
"CENTER"

①

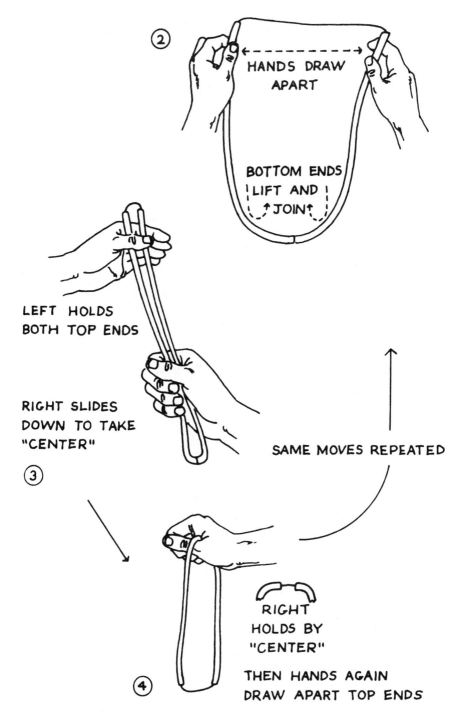

② HANDS DRAW APART

BOTTOM ENDS LIFT AND JOIN

LEFT HOLDS BOTH TOP ENDS

RIGHT SLIDES DOWN TO TAKE "CENTER"

③

SAME MOVES REPEATED

RIGHT HOLDS BY "CENTER"

THEN HANDS AGAIN DRAW APART TOP ENDS

④

continued on next page . . .

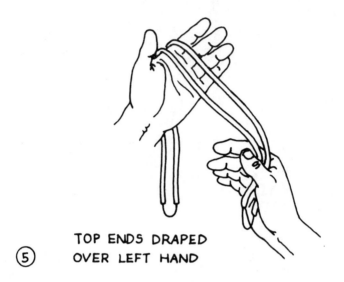

TOP ENDS DRAPED
(5)   OVER LEFT HAND

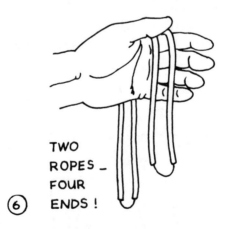

TWO
ROPES –
FOUR
(6)   ENDS !

Bring the two ropes together at the bottom of the loop of thread, with their lower ends butted against each other to form what would be the center of a single length of rope. Place the rope on your table with that "center" toward the back.

What you do

With your left hand palm-down, pick up the centered ends of the rope and close your fingers into a fist around them. Hold those ends within your hands as if you held a single rope at the center, with the other two ends hanging down at the bottom. Hold the rope up high to show it, as you say, "It is important to hold the rope at its exact center."

Bring your right hand to your left hand. Take one end in each hand, holding the ends upright so they can be seen above the hands, and spread your hands apart as far as the thread will allow. This should be done quickly, but smoothly and gently, as you say, "I mean, if the two *ends* were at the *top*, then the *center* wouldn't be there because. . . ."

Drawing your hands apart visibly lifts the two bottom ends up against each other so they appear to join together. You are now holding the separate top ends of what still seems to be a single rope, but with its center suddenly at the bottom instead of at the top. (You will find that if you give the whole rope a little downward shake as you draw your hands apart, the bottom ends will butt together more evenly.) Pretending to be confused by what has happened, you say, "It's all upside down. Let me start again."

Bring your right hand to your left hand. Place the rope end your right hand is holding beside the end in your left hand and hold both ends with your left hand. Immediately run your right hand down the rope to the bottom. Close your right hand into a fist around the "center" that is now at the bottom, holding those two bottom ends inside your right hand.

Now, lift your right hand high and at the same time drop the ends from your left hand, so that they fall to hang separately at the bottom. As at the start, you seem to be holding a single rope at its center, but this time with your right hand. "If I hold the center at the top," you say, "then naturally the two ends are at the bottom."

Bring your left hand to your right hand, take one top end in each hand, hold them upright, and draw your hands apart as before. Once again, the bottom ends are drawn together so the rope seems to have turned itself upside down, with its center at the bottom and ends at the top. "That's still upside down!" you say, as you jokingly suggest that members of the audience should stand on their heads. "No, wait—I've got it now."

Put both top ends into your left hand to hold them a moment. Close your right hand around both strands of rope and *quickly* run it down to the bottom. Take the bottom ends in your right hand and drop the top ends from your left hand. Turn your left palm toward you and open your thumb and fingers wide. Drape the center of both strands over the top of your left hand, so the top ends hang down separately over the back of that hand, but keep your right hand closed around the bottom ends it is holding.

"If I have two ends at the top and if I also have two ends at the bottom ..." As you speak, secretly spread the two bottom ends in the right hand with your thumb, so they will hang straight and about an inch apart, not curled together, and then let those ends drop and remove your right hand. "... then I must have *four* ends." Instead of "one" rope, you now have two pieces draped side by side over your left hand, with four ends hanging down. Turn your left hand to show it back and front. "And so I have!"

Take the ropes together with your right hand. "But now, I don't know where the *center* went," you say, as you toss them aside on the table. "And *that* doesn't make any sense at all!"